Howard the Duck

. . . Howard heard a gunshot.

He started, flapped, squawked ('SQUAWKK!')
and whirled. He flattened himself against the window,
cop-show style, and looked frantically about for cover.
He was unarmed and defenceless, they'd doubled the
limit, and it would hurt . . .

'I'm not takin' any chances,' Howard muttered.
With a fearful look in both directions, he grabbed his
bag and ran. When he came to an alley, he ducked in.

On the run from everyone and no one. Surrounded
by an alien species on a planet he'd never even heard
of. 'This is it,' Howard thought, pausing for breath
against a cold wall. 'This is the perfect metaphor for
the duck condition.' Estranged from himself and mad
at everyone else, imprisoned for no crime, in a place he
had nothing to do with.

Howard the Duck; trapped in a world he never
made . . .

Ellis Weiner

Howard the Duck

FONTANA/Collins

A continental edition first issued
by Fontana Paperbacks 1986
HOWARD THE DUCK: TM and © 1986 Marvel Comics Group,
a division of Cadence Industries Corporation

Made and printed in Great Britain by
William Collins Sons & Co. Ltd, Glasgow

One

THE UNIVERSE.

A BOILING CHAOS OF MATTER AND ENERGY. WHERE BILLIONS AND BILLIONS –

Hold it. 'Boiling chaos?' 'Billions and billions?' The bill of fare announces Howard the Duck and you're playing Carl Sagan? Who let you on this page? What is this? Who are you?

I AM THE VOICE OF THE GREATER COSMO-LOGICAL CONTEXT.

You mean 'God'.

WELL . . . NOT TO BE IMMODEST . . . BUT I AM THE VOICE THAT SPEAKS ON BEHALF OF THE INFINITE . . . THE VOICE THAT SAYS, FOR THE AGES, THAT-WHICH-CANNOT-BE-SAID.

Uh-huh. And do you –

IT IS I WHOSE PEAR-SHAPED TONES EN-COMPASS GALAXIES . . . I WHO INVOKE THE EXTREMITIES OF COSMIC BOUNDLESSNESS. OMNISCIENT I IT IS WHO USHERS PUNY STU-PID YOU INTO THE AWESOME DOMAIN OF ETERNITY.

Be nice.

LISTEN, AND LEARN OF THE DESTINY OF WORLDS. HEAR, AND GRASP THE ULTIMATE ACTS OF CREATION AND DESTRUCTION. ATTEND, AND ADMIRE THE VOICE THAT LAUNCHED A THOUSAND IDENTICAL

DOCUMENTARIES ... ABOUT ORVILLE AND WILBUR, GODDARD AND VON BRAUN, SPUTNIK AND SCHMUTNIK AND 'THE MIRACLE OF FLIGHT'.

Are you the guy who says things like: 'Ever since he first gazed in wonder towards the heavens –'

'– MAN HAS YEARNED TO FLY.' YES. I IT IS WHO SAYS SUCH STUFF AS LIKE THAT.

I thought you sounded familiar.

I AM MORE THAN FAMILIAR. I AM UBIQUITOUS. INNUMERABLE ARE THE SECOND-RATE SCIENCE FICTION STORIES TOLD IN VOICES APING MINE. UNCOUNTABLE THE S.F. MOVIES INTRO'D OR OUTRO'D BY FACSIMILES OF ME. NO ASTRONOMY SHOW ON TELEVISION GETS AIRED WITHOUT I SAY SO.

Which brings us at last to Howard the Duck –?

I AM THAT VOICE – THAT VOICE OF VOICES – OF WHICH ROD SERLING'S ('YOU UNLOCK THIS DOOR WITH THE KEY OF IMAGINATION ...') AND WILLIAM SHATNER'S ('SPACE ... THE FINAL FRONTIER ...') AND THAT GUY ON THE OUTER LIMITS ('THERE IS NOTHING WRONG WITH YOUR TELEVISION SET ...') ARE BUT FEEBLE IMITATIONS.

All right, all right, I'm convinced. You're God.

YOU FLATTER ME. BUT VERY WELL. LET IT BE SO. I AM GOD.

Fine. But I'm the narrator. So shut up and let's get started.

Howard, a duck on a world of ducks, got home from work one afternoon, beat.

THE UNIVERSE.
A BOILING CHAOS OF MATTER AND ENERGY.
WHERE BILLIONS AND BILLIONS OF STARS RAGE
IN CEASELESS, SILENT FURY. WITHIN THIS
THROBBING ELECTROMAGNETIC PANDEMO-
NIUM, ALONG THAT REAL BUT NONEXISTENT
BORDER BETWEEN NOTHINGNESS AND SOME-
THINGNESS, TIME ITSELF IS UNLEASHED:
RELENTLESS, MYSTER –

He threw his briefcase on the couch and trooped off into
the kitchen for a beer. The place was a disaster – unwashed
dishes in the sink, yesterday's leftover Le Canard Gourmet
Frozen Vegetable Medley in A Light Creme Sauce still in the
pot, a half-empty bag of Mallardmars on the table. Howard,
from ducklinghood hectored by his mother to be neat, had
been a slob ever since leaving the nest. He barely noticed the
mess.

– IOUS, UNSTOPPABLE TIME, FLOWING
THROUGH THIS HALF-EMPTY BAG OF ELECTRO-
. . . THIS . . .
I'LL START AGAIN.
THE UNIVERSE.
THROUGHOUT THE STAGGERING INFINITUDE
OF SPACE-TIME, WHERE COUNTLESS GALAXIES
CAREEN AT UNIMAGINEABLE VELOCITIES
THROUGH AN AIRLESS, FRIGID VOID, MATTER
COMBINES WITH ENERGY TO FORM . . . LIFE!
THE MIRACLE OF LIFE! AMOEBAE! BEAGLES!
EVERYTHING! AND FROM LIFE ITSELF: THE
MULTIPL –

Howard was not only tired, he was irritable, and assailed
by that almost nauseating sense of futility and waste that,
sooner or later, descends on almost everyone the moment
they perceive – if only for a second – how pointless and dumb
their jobs really are.

He had spent the whole day arguing about the Quacker Oats account. The idea was to sell oatmeal to grown ducks and drakes. The trouble was, people usually associated hot cereals with when they were ducklings. Now the client wanted to reach the hard-waddling corporate types, the Directed Upward Career Klass everyone was calling (or pretending to be tired of calling) the DUCKIES.

Howard had come up with a pretty good slogan: 'You don't really have it all if you don't have Quacker Oats for breakfast.' A little clumsy, but it did manage to use several of the key concepts. But his boss had nixed it and chosen a different one – 'Quacker Oats. Because you're not a sitting duck.'

'Aw, come on, Don,' Howard had said. 'That doesn't make any sense. It says, "eat oatmeal because you're not an easy target." It's paranoid and sleazy at the same time.'

'Technically, Howard, verbally speaking, that may be semantically true,' Howard's boss had said. He was the sort of middle-management chap who happily conceded every point you made, because his mind was already closed. 'But it reads kinetic. I'm not a sitting duck means, I'm a duck who's not sitting. Right? I'm not sitting around on my tail feathers. I'm going. I'm flying. I'm an on-the-move type of individual, right? I'm going Up! Up! Up! It reads what I call "goal-oriented" because it's a situation of Hey, look out. I'm happening. I'm going for so-called "it," quote-unquote. I appreciate the rewards that come from living very, very well. I'm the duck of the 80s.'

Howard wasn't sure what all this had to do with oatmeal.

– THE MULTIPLICITY OF OATMEAL ... OF LIFE-FORMS ... A DAZZLING VARIETY OF LIVING ORGANISMS EVOLVING ON MILLIONS OF PLANETS THROUGHOUT THE COSMOS. THE ENDLESS DRAMA OF EVOLUTION: SIMPLE ORGANISMS BECOMING COMPLEX, ATTAINING

CONSCIOUSNESS . . . GROWING . . . CREATING
SOCIETIES . . . CONSTRUCTING CIVILIZATIONS
OF REMARKABLE SOPHISTI –

Howard flipped open a bottle of St Pauli Gull and headed
back to the living room. Maybe something decent was on
TV. But the first few turns of the dial revealed the same old
late-afternoon junk:

– a re-run of *Drakenet*, with Jack Webb: 'Just tell us the
quacks, Shorty.'

'Fat chance, Fryday . . .'

– a hospital scene from *Call My Children*: 'I'm afraid your
star witness is . . . blind, Kimberly.'

'This duck? Blind? Oh my god, Bill –!'

– the spy movie, *Platypussy*: 'It appears I've under-
estimate you, Mr James Pond . . .'

He kept changing channels until he came to a basketball
pre-game show. Chick Hearn was interviewing Larry Bird.
'Hey, great!' Howard said, and sat back and sipped his beer.

It was about then that his chair started to move.

-CATION. AND AMONG THIS INFINITE, MUL-
TIFA –
REALLY?

It was brief, a sort of shiver. Howard thought it must have
been caused by a passing truck, or one of his neighbours
dropping something heavy. It stopped after a second, so he
looked back at the TV. Hearn was asking Bird how he liked
playing against Kareem Abdul-Jabarnswallow.

The chair started to move again.

This time it began as a fine, subtle vibration, but quickly
grew into a bone-rattling shake. 'I'm dreamin',' Howard told
himself. 'I musta fallen asleep in front of the tube . . .'

But if Howard was dreaming, so was his furniture – whatever was causing the chair to rock around on its four feet, in a
kind of stationary gallop, was also making the living room go

nuts. A lamp fell off the side table and crashed to the floor. A bowling trophy tumbled off the shuddering TV. A vase and some framed pictures (his parents; Howard on stage at Folk City; Howard looking glum on the first day of med. school) plummeted off the mantelpiece. 'It's an earthquake!' he thought. 'Gotta get out of this maniac chair –' He leaned forward –

To the extent that chairs are able to have ideas, Howard's chair had other ideas. It tipped; he fell back. Then, with its duck passenger helplessly off-balance, the chair shot backwards. Howard grabbed onto the vinyl-upholstered arms and hooked his legs around the front, as what until now had been an ordinary La-Z-Bird lounger roared like a rocket sled smack into the living room wall in an explosion of wood and plaster.

He had shut his eyes for the impact. Now, when he opened them, he discovered that, in the comfort of his own easy chair, he had paid a visit to his neighbours. The chair had smashed through his wall into the drab, stuffy dwelling of Herb and Edna next door.

For one suspended moment Howard was treated to a glimpse of unselfconscious anatidaean domesticity – i.e., a nice quiet duck evening at home. Herb was on the living room couch, reading the paper, his webbed feet up; Edna was taking something from the refrigerator in the kitchen. Then the chair zoomed through, sending tables banging and rugs flying, smashing lamps and mirrors, leaving a wake of scattered newspapers and flapping magazines. Herb squawked, 'What th' –?' and Edna screamed. Howard croaked 'Help!' and was gone –

– crashing through a wall, into the hallway, barrelling along, pinned to the chair as though on a rollercoaster. Doors flashed past; ahead of him, the far wall and its one (closed) window drew rapidly nearer. The chair felt like it had engines strapped to its back. Then he was at the wall. He braced himself – and burst through, out into the placid evening. 'Oh cripes,' he said out loud. He curled into a ball and waited, cringing, for the inevitable fall to the ground.

It never came. The chair flew off into the sky and Up! Up! Up! He may have been a sitting duck, but he was definitely on the move. He was flying, he was going for it. On the street below – far below – shoppers with bags, cabbies leaning out their car windows, kids tossing balls, cops on the beat, and other assorted fowl looked up in curiosity and disbelief as Howard and his easy chair soared off into the shimmering night sky like a meteorite in reverse. He was happening. He was kinetic. He was the duck of the 80s.

EXACTLY. WHICH BRINGS US BACK TO –

THE UNIVERSE! WITH ITS VAST ARRAY OF PLANETS AND LIFE-FORMS.

IN THIS INFINITY OF TIME AND SPACE AND MATTER AND ENERGY AND SO FORTH, ALL POSSIBLE WORLDS EXIST. WHAT IS AIRY FANTASY ON ONE IS ROCK-FIRM REALITY ON ANOTHER. ON ONE PLANET, MEN ARE MEN. ON ANOTHER, THEY ARE LARGE GLASSES OF MILK.

AND ON STILL ANOTHER – ON HOWARD'S WORLD – MEN ARE D –

Howard's last glimpse of Duck World came as his chair suddenly dropped away, like a rocket's booster burning out. It fell off, but he kept going, faster than ever, arms flailing, through the great vacuum. Below him, the planet of his birth turned slowly, a blueish ball about the size of an orange and getting smaller every second. He could just make out the continent of Daffrica. Thousands of stars now surrounded him, bright, fiery pinpoints –

EXCUSE ME. 'BRIGHT, FIERY PINPOINTS?' 'THOUSANDS OF STARS?' PLEASE. WHEN DESCRIBING THE INEFFABLE MYSTERIES OF THE COSMOS, ALWAYS RELY ON A PROFESSIONAL.

STARS! THOUSANDS OF BRIGHT, FIERY

11

PINPOINTS, ASWIRL IN THE NEBULAE AND CLUSTERS AND GASEOUS GALAXY FORMATIONS OF THE VAST, FAST, GHASTLY REACHES OF IN-TERSTELLAR SP –

– as he hurtled towards what he could dimly sense was some unknown but profound fate. Miraculously, he was able to breathe. Neither the intense heat nor the absolute cold of space had any effect. He could even, against all the rules of physics, hear things. What he heard sounded very much like a duck screaming ('Jee-zus KWAAAAK!') his head off.

'Gotta get a grip,' he muttered. 'Can't panic.'

Howard tried to get some perspective on what was happening. Actually, he shouldn't have been too surprised at all this. Being plucked out of his home, when all he'd been doing was going about his business, not bothering anybody or demanding anything – it was the story of his life. The world took pleasure in sneaking up on you and finding new and creative ways to make you miserable. One minute you're sipping a beer in your living room, the next minute you're on a chair zooming through outer space. Boy, was that typical.

Plus, who needed it? Sure, the scenery was nice – giant pinwheeling galaxies drifting past his widened eyes, flaring comets and sizzling meteors and other space fireworks diving and flaring and exploding out to infinity, and all. But how would he ever get back home?

'Plus, it's kinda lonely out here,' Howard murmured.

OF COURSE IT'S LONELY. IT'S ... THE UNIVERSE!

'Then what am I doin' out in the middle of it?' Howard said, not sure whom he was talking to but glad to make some conversation. 'I didn't ask to be here. All I wanted was to have a brew and wait for *Quacker John M.D.* What's wrong with that?'

NOTHING. BUT YOUR EXPERIENCE REFLECTS

ONE OF THE PRINCIPAL LAWS OF ... THE UNIVERSE. SOME DUCKS ARE BORN GREAT. SOME ACHIEVE GREATNESS. SOME HAVE GREATNESS THRUST UPON THEM. AND SOME ...

Howard waited a moment. He was in no mood for dramatic pauses. 'Yeah? Some what?'

SOME DUCKS END UP IN THE WRONG PLACE AT THE WRONG TIME.

'Great. Thanks.'

Howard hurtled on. He decided he could live without the interior conversation between himself and whatever Cosmic Spirit or alter-ego was coming back with such lousy answers. There was only one question that concerned him as he whizzed through the limitless unfathomable blah-blah of Space.

Where would it all end?

Apparently on an opaline blue-green planet, sheathed in swirling white clouds, about the size of a grapefruit and getting steadily larger. Howard stared. The planet approached – basketball size, then big as a beachball, then the giant in-your-face size of that huge canvas monster-ball they used to kick around in high school gym class on rainy days. (It was bigger than the students. Once it had hit him in the bill, knocking him down and drawing blood. Other ducks had laughed, but he'd felt heroic.)

It then occurred to him that flying off into thin air was one thing, but smashing head-first onto terra firma was another. And he wasn't even slowing down; he could feel his velocity increasing, his body caught in this world's gravitational pull like a fish on a line. The big blue planet began to reel him in.

'Hey, enough's enough now, okay?' he said aloud. No answer. 'I mean, fun's fun, and all . . .' Nothing. He swung into an orbit around the immense blue globe, which now turned lazily beneath him and filled his entire field of vision. It was a pretty thing, but he wasn't sure he wanted to go

13

ploughing head-first into it. But then, it wasn't up to him. None of this was.

'HELP!'

He was still yelling when his orbit decayed, and he fell.

Plummeting through the planet's atmosphere felt like sinking deeper and deeper into a pool filled with soapsuds. The air got thicker. He could actually feel it on his hands. Amazingly though he didn't burn up. Still shouting ('YAAAAHHHHHH!') he broke through the clouds and could see, below, a sprawling, dark mass of land. In a minute, between screams, he got close enough to make out a million tiny flecks of light. It was inhabited! He was heading for the centre of an odd-shaped continent, and five black, shimmering bodies of water.

'What if it's not water!' he squawked. 'What if it's science fiction stuff, like methane! Or ammonia! It could be anything! Those lakes could be filled with sangria, for all I know! This is outer space!' Howard, who didn't care for wine-based fruit beverages, blanched.

Nonsense? Sure – but this whole event was crazy. And if there was a purpose to this exercise, it escaped him.

PURPOSE? DON'T MAKE ME LAUGH. THERE IS NO PURPOSE IN . . . THE U –

Howard saw, to his horror, that he was heading, not for a nice wet lake or ocean, nor even for the dubious mercies of a snowbank or forest, but directly towards a city made entirely of stone, brick, concrete and steel. He was going to land smack on his little duck's ass. And it was going to smart.

'I wanna meet the guy who's in charge of this!' he squawked. 'I demand an explanation!'

It was all he could manage. A vast landscape of buildings and roads was rushing up at him. He could identify moving vehicles, apartment houses, blocks lined with street lights, individual houses and garages, playing fields, factories – it seemed like a good idea to start screaming again.

'HEEEEELLLLLPPP!'

Howard crashed through a billboard reading CLEVELAND VAN & STORAGE and sent up a shower of sparks, splinters, and feathers. His momentum, which was prodigious, sent him ever onward; he bounced off a water tank, flew off the edge of a building, caromed off a wooden overhang, and slammed into a trash dumpster with a loud, reverberant BONG. He came to rest in an alley, on a dilapidated easy chair set out that evening for the trash men.

The duck had landed.

Howard warily opened his eyes. His normal duckly tenor was a soft whimper. 'This isn't fair.'

TRUE. BUT THUS HAS IT ALWAYS BEEN. AND THUS IT SHALL REMAIN.

FOR THIS IS . . . THE UNIVERSE.

THERE'S NO OTHER PLACE LIKE IT.

Howard looked around without moving. He had thought the line was, 'There's no place like home.' But this was some other place. He sat up and, aching, weary, exhausted, and in a bad mood, sighed, 'Oy.'

YOU CAN SAY THAT AGAIN, HOWARD.

Two

Howard dragged himself up in the huge, lumpy chair. He was tense with conflicting desires – within his semi-cute duck's body rampaging hormones debated which option to elect of his squawk-or-walk response. On the one hand, he was eager to get up and look around – for safety's sake, if not out of brute curiosity. On the other, he had just flown in from another star system, and boy, were his arms tired. So there was an argument to be made for resting, and restoring his energies.

But who could relax? He'd landed in a foul-smelling alley near a trash bin as big as a railroad car. Wan street lights, bare bulbs, some harsh red neon: the place was gloomy, the walls all around him dark with threatening shadows. A block away, a strange sort of factory was the source of a loud, grinding, shrieking, crashing noise.

Of course, exploration would almost certainly be dangerous. Judging from the size of this chair, he had landed on a world of giants. He might venture three steps out into the street, and be crushed flat by one of their cruel, sportive children.

'I'm in what's called a no-win situation,' Howard reflected. 'An' I didn't even ask to play!' What to do? He sought (in vain) a comfortable position on the chair, and awaited inspiration.

COVERAGE-IN-DEPTH INSERT 1
Comparison and Contrast of Leisure Chairs on Duck World and Earth

Perhaps the highest expression of a society's values and beliefs can be found in its leisure chairs. Perhaps it can't. Indeed, perhaps a study of a society's chairs yields little more than the knowledge of how individuals in that society sit around. In any case, the fact that Howard the Duck's epic trek begins in one such chair and ends in another is, if not significant, certainly worth a few remarks.

We begin by comparing the chairs. Howard's, a La-Z-Bird Model #12-A, was a basic recliner. Its cover was of vinyl, in a dark green entitled 'Forest Glade'. Its cushions were filled with the space-age material Miracle-Lon-Endura-Tron-Textra-Phirm-Z. Its footrest swung up and out as its exclusive Tilt-A-Swiv feature provided the ultimate in almost-horizontal duck comfort.

Granted: it looked more enticing than it actually was. When Howard reclined in it, the chair transported his head too far back to see the TV, dragged his hands too far from his eyes to read and held his entire body not quite flat enough for sleeping. Sitting in its half-way position, he could neither eat nor drink in it. After a few minutes of semi-luxurious stretching out, Howard usually felt cramped and captive, served up supine in the palm of a giant.

The armchair he landed on in the alley was a Grand Rapids FurnCo Mis-Ter Sof-Touch Model S-114. It did not swivel, and lacked a retractable footrest. It was in point of fact an ordinary stuffed chair, its upholstery a mix of cotton and polyester, its padding Type 3 of Toxichem's Syn-the-tique Cot-'N'-Ite-EZ-Dura-Sopht Fiberific Blend. The central molecule of this brutally synthetic fibre was eight feet long and glowed in the dark. This was the same stuffing/batting/padding material Toxichem would seek permission to sell in Central Africa as a filling for candy bars.

Thus the two chairs, one (Howard's, designed and manufactured on Duck World) capable of movement and adjustment of orientation, the other (human, designed and manufactured on Earth) fixed. From these simple facts we may draw some immediate and startling conclusions:

1) Ducks may assume a variety of physical positions, but humans are incapable of motion. Only a species of creatures that moved would find it evolutionarily necessary to create tilting furniture. Ducks, as is already known, have legs, which they use for resting on the footrest mechanism of their lounge chairs. Human beings, in contrast, have chairs, which they use for remaining stationary. In light of this fact, the development of human civilization strikes one more forcibly than ever as nothing short of astounding.

2) Ducks desire the ultimate in luxurious elegant comfort and are willing to spend a few more dollars in order to obtain the quality home furnishings of their dreams. Humans, meanwhile, are cheapskates, who buy trash.

3) Duck World is a planet of civilized individuals voluntarily assembled into a democratic republic in which the rule of the representative few over the many has its origins in the consent of the majority and rests on the guarantee of the individual's right to sit in a reclining lounge chair. Earth, in contrast, is a crazy place where anything can happen.

No wonder Howard will have a hard time of it.

That hard time began almost immediately, in the form of four huge, menacing natives.

They saw Howard just as he saw them, and moved slowly into the alley staring at him in wonder – at least, it looked like they were registering, around the makeup, scars, and tattoos on their faces, 'wonder' – and cutting off any escape. Howard had expected this planet's life-forms to be ugly, but this quartet was really more horrible than necessary.

For one thing, they had no feathers at all, just some thin, brown moss-like growth on their heads. Their bills were barely worthy of the name. And it was hard to see how they managed to stand upright, since their feet were, compared to a duck's ordinary webbed ones, tiny.

18

Their clothes looked suitably odd, too. Leather jackets studded with spikes and metal buttons, chains, amulets – Howard guessed they belonged to some kind of warrior class, armed for battle. Then he took a wild guess.

'Are you the police?' he asked hopefully.

Two of them laughed. A third sneered, 'Yeah, right . . .'

'Oh, God,' another moaned. 'I'm like so ripped, man, I'm seeing this talking like duck, okay?'

They moved toward him. Howard felt his heart suddenly start thudding in his chest. This was a civilization of barbarian killers! These creatures probably ate ducks! He struggled to get up and run, but his foot was caught in one of the springs protruding from the chair. The four giants loomed over him, blocking out the light. He could hear the creak of their leather garments as one of them bent down and picked him up –!

The creature's touch was surprisingly gentle. Howard found himself lifted face to gruesome face with this leering featherless biped, who turned to his fellow barbarians and said, 'Hey, man, like I just picked up this talking duck, okay?'

'Big deal, man,' another said.

'So like now what do I do?'

'Like eat it for Thanksgiving, man.'

'That's a turkey, jerk-face.'

'You're a turkey, scuzz-brain.'

Did everyone on this planet talk like this? Howard began to fear that he'd landed on a world of mental defectives. One of these creatures now leaned close to Howard's face and said, 'Hey, like, Polly want a, you know, cracker, man?'

'The name's Howard,' the duck said. 'And that's not a bad idea. I could use a bite.'

'Let's give him to Bender, man,' one of them said.

The one holding Howard laughed. 'O great. Bender'll freak.'

Howard had no idea what they were talking about. But ap-

19

parently they thought the prospect of Bender freaking was a good thing. The four trooped off towards the building from which the noise had seemed to double in volume. The one carrying Howard held him under his arm like a football.

'Maybe I oughta resist,' Howard thought, as he was transported out of the alley towards the unrelenting din. 'I mean, am I just gonna take this lying down?' On Duck World he had seen enough movies and TV shows to know that a red-blooded duck was supposed to be heroic. You didn't have to be a Macho Mallard to be aware of the fact that society expected you to fight back – and win.

But that was fiction! Adventure stuff, cheap melodramas and revenge fantasies, written by birds who probably (like Howard) had never been in a fight in their lives. Did real adults actually haul off and sock other real adults? Should he try to fight back against these creatures now? Said who? And besides, one puny Howard against these four chain-studded giants? The line between a courageous effort at defiant self-defence, and being smashed into duck confit against a wall, was a fine one. But it wasn't invisible.

Still, that didn't keep Howard from feeling doubly miserable – not only afraid of what might happen, but actually embarrassed to be so helpless. 'Wauugh, this is humiliatin',' he thought.

The 'factory' from which all the 'noise' had been blaring turned out to be some kind of night club. A crowd of people swarmed around the doorway. Inside Howard could see, from his captive's elevation, people seated at tables in the darkness, and a brightly-lit stage beyond. Howard's four captors greeted a throng of their fellows, all wearing leather, studs, little knives, and chains. Many of them had black makeup on their eyes. Howard wasn't sure he wanted to be around when one of these individuals 'freaked'.

'Yo, Bender,' one of his escorts called.

A truly frightening man, jostling and snorting with the crowd, turned. 'Yeah?'

He looked ugly, which Howard did not take personally. Like any enlightened duck, he tried not to be judgmental about personal appearance – after all, Howard knew he himself was no Bird Reynolds. But this creature was distinguished by more than just a hook nose, massive pugnacious chin and beady eyes. He also looked mean. And that could have a very real effect on Howard's level of personal comfort. The fowl's heart began to thump again, just as he found himself thrust into the brute's arms.

'Here ya go, Frankenweenie,' one of the four said. 'We finally found ya a date!'

'Hey, what –'

They shoved Bender (and his armful of live duck) in through the door. Dozens of these warrior-natives were standing around in the darkness, craning towards the front of the room and shouting over the searing, booming noise. Howard followed their eyes and saw, on a small stage in bright lights, what he presumed to be females.

There were four of them, all playing what looked like instruments and producing what therefore must be music. Front and centre, at the microphone, was a very striking creature, all curves and hot energy. She wasn't exactly Howard's type (for that matter, she wasn't exactly Howard's species), but he couldn't help noticing her.

Bender looked at the bundle of feathers and fear that had been placed in his arms. 'This . . . this looks like some kinda duck!'

'Like brilliant, Sherlock,' somebody said.

('Gotta make conversation,' Howard told himself. 'Maybe he'll simmer down.') He tried an innocent, I'm-no-threat smile and said, 'Bender Frankenweenie . . . that's a beautiful name. Mine's Howard.'

'Hah?'

'Hey, are you guys nuts?' A mammoth bruiser in a sports coat rumbled up. Howard, still in Bender's arms, felt as though he were surrounded by redwoods wearing makeup.

'You want us to lose our licence? Costume or no costume, NO KIDS ALLOWED!' He grabbed Howard, hoisted him up high over his head, and bulled his way through the throng.

Simple abuse was one thing; being mistaken for a baby goat was downright insulting. 'Who's a kid?!' Howard quacked. 'I'm a duck, ya big bully!'

'You're history now, pal,' the man said, and flung the squawking, flapping Howard ('WAAAAK!') out of the door like a bag of potatoes.

Was ever a duck so abused? Howard bounced off the roof of a car and caromed back into the alley from which he thought he'd been rescued. He landed in a shopping trolley, and was duly clobbered on the head by its unfolding infant seat. (A metal plate on it was printed with words suggesting an uneasy compromise between the P.R. endearing – THIS SPOT RESERVED FOR FUTURE FOODVILLE CUSTOMERS. – and the Federally-mandated – DO NOT LEAVE YOUR CHILD UNATTENDED.)

The trolley rolled into a ragged creature rooting through a line of trash cans. The woman – it was probably a woman – leaped up and shrieked.

'Mugger!' she shouted, pointing. 'Thief! Degenerate!'

('How come,' Howard wondered, 'people with barely ten words in their vocabulary always seem to know how to say "degenerate"?') 'Duck!' he corrected her. 'Duck!'

'You duck, you little degenerate!' The woman grabbed the strap of her bulging handbag and began flailing. She may have been filthy, crazy and in rags, but she was strong – the bag felt like it was filled with rocks. (It was.) Howard warded off the blows as best he could, leaped from the trolley, and waddled for all he was worth down the alley. This was a terrible planet and he was sorry he ever came here –

He heard a noise.

The stabbing beams of two searing white lights struck him smack in the eyes. The largest, loudest object Howard had ever seen had appeared at the end of the alley. It was moving towards him with an ear-splitting roar made doubly deafening by the echo-chamber narrowness and hard brick walls. Howard made full use of the one second he had to leap aside, as a vehicle the size of a house, bearing the sign CLEVELAND REFUSE CARTERS, INC. ('We Never Refuse Refuse'), rumbled past.

He had landed in a doorway. It was dank, dark, cold. And he was – like Duck World itself in *Close Encounters of the Bird Kind* – not alone. Howard reached a tentative hand behind him (actually turning around and looking was out of the question), and felt something he would have been forced to describe as meaty. Like, say, a leg. He moved his hand up and confirmed that yes, indeed, this was a leg. Howard was no expert on this planet's zoology, but even he knew that the leg would most likely be attached to a person –

'OH, GOD! IT TOUCHED ME! UGGH!' The screamer, owner of the leg in question, was a young woman, who until that moment had been in a close embrace with a young man in the doorway.

'Sorry, sorry,' Howard said. 'Nothing personal –'

'What the hell –?' her companion said.

'OH, YUCK! IT TALKS! GROSS!'

'Hey, gimme a break!' Howard pleaded. 'I'm new in town –'

'KILL IT, BILLY! FILTHY ALLEY DUCK –!'

Billy grabbed a piece of wood and swung. It smashed into splinters against the wall. Howard, for want of a better term, ran like hell.

He was getting tired. There had to be more to life than hustling back and forth in a cold, miserable alley. Even on this planet. On the other hand, maybe the whole planet was one big alley. Maybe things never got any better here. What if this was the best they had! Suppose this was their swellest resort! Their equivalent of Acapoultry! Okay, fine, if that was the case. Who was Howard to judge? Cultures and civilizations were all different. These people probably liked dank streets, garbage, deafening noise, and maniacs.

'To each his own,' Howard thought, panting. 'Can I go now?'

A new noise rumbled into earshot: a sputtering, angry growl, like the sound of ten thousand snoring rhinos. Howard beheld a line of electric lights mounted on fat, squat motorcycles, atop of which rode a squad of plug-uglies in leather and beards. They swept forward down the alley towards the hapless bird, who looked wildly around in noisy ('KWAAAAAKK!') desperation for a way out. There were no doorways, no trash cans, no windows, nothing. Howard the Duck faced imminent extinction.

He spied a chain hanging overhead. Evidently it operated some sort of loading dock for one of the buildings. Howard jumped up high. The chain was inches from his hand. He grabbed it. It gave a bit, then held firm. He held himself there, suspended, while the herd of mechanical beasts rampaged below.

He was safe. He allowed himself a discreet chuckle of triumph. 'Not bad,' he thought. The chain broke.

Howard landed on the handlebars of the last bike. Its rider, a man the size (to other men) of a coffee-and-chicken-soup vending machine and (to Howard) of a monster, had a grizzled beard, eyebrows like porcupines, and the crazed leer of a maladjusted sociopath. Who knows, he may have been very nice. On his jacket was the emblem of SATAN'S SLAVES. A woman with dyed yellow hair rode behind him. She looked exactly like he did, except for the beard. She had no beard. She had a moustache.

They were moving along at a rapid clip. The biker looked startled. Howard tried to soothe the mood. 'Hi,' he said – always a safe opening. 'Say, are you ready for an amazing story?'

'WASTE THE LITTLE GEEK!' screamed the woman behind the man. 'I SAID WASTE 'IM, BEAR, WASTE 'IM!'

24

'Now there's no need to waste anybody, Bear,' Howard began. (He knew how to talk to lunatics. Didn't he work in advertising? Hadn't he dealt with the great Waddlemire himself, who made Bear look as mild and reasonable as Duckminster Fuller?) 'You see, I was sitting at home, in my living room, having a beer. And, then, well, my chair started to move –'

Bear growled what sounded like, 'Kravzztvvsrfrtz,' – high eloquence for him – and swiped at the blabbing bird with his studded leather bracelet. With this not unagonizing smash to the noggin Howard flew off towards a trash can like a duck in a demented high school physics problem. ('Duck H, riding bike A at velocity v in direction d, acquires force x in direction y by being slugged by Biker B after being called geek by Mama M. Chart vector of duck's motion and compute impact of H's head-first crash-landing in stationary garbage can G.')

The bikes roared off into the night. The noise from the club abated for a few minutes. In the unfamiliar silence, two wide eyes rose from the depths of the can. They peered in unblinking shock around the alley. Their owner, a duck from another planet, did not trust the quiet.

He spied the can's top nearby on the ground, grabbed it, and sank down into the can, slamming the lid after him like the submarine crew battening down the hatches in Howard's favourite war movie, *Fowl Fathom Five*. He was alone, at last, in the safety and quiet and comforting dark of a garbage can. It reminded him of something he'd read in college, back when English majors roamed the planet. *Kwakk's Last Tape? Wading for Godot?* One of those.

'Whatever,' he sighed. He decided not to think about it. He was free, at last, to do the one thing he had been craving to do for about an hour. He passed out cold.

He passed out 'coldly?'

Not Howard. He passed out cold.

Three

Beverly Switzler and the other women of Cherry Bomb were well acquainted with the First Law of Playing Dives: Secure your due emolument prior to the commencement of your professional activities, lest you be unfairly denied it subsequent to rendering services.

In other words: Get your pay before you play, or it's no dough when it's time to go.

Clubs expected every band they hired to be 'professional', but the owners and managers of these grunge-holes were pros at one thing only – feeling sorry for themselves. Ask for your money after a five-hour gig, and all they handed you was 'Gimme a break' and 'We didn't do enough business.' These guys made the Mafia look like a reputable financial institution. Meanwhile you were stiffed. What could you do? Unplay the music and take it all back?

So Cherry Bomb should have known better when their so-called 'manager,' Ginger Moss, asked them to perform without any cash up front. Bev couldn't even remember at this point why they'd signed with him. Probably they'd been impressed by his limo.

'What am I supposed to tell my landlord?' K.C., their bass player, grumbled.

'Tell him Ginger says we're gonna be stars some day,' Caldonia said. She dropped her drumsticks into her stick bag. 'Star bag ladies, probably.'

'Where is Ginger?' Beverly asked. She had already packed her guitar. Not having anything else to do, she was getting mad. 'I'm gonna read him the riot act.'

Ronette, the rhythm guitarist, said, 'Better move fast. Old Ginger just split.'

'Come on.'

The three others followed Beverly through the club, ignoring the lame pickup lines and halfhearted hoots from the few punks who were left – the ones too wired or bored or messed up to go home, but who were still conscious. Sure enough, out on the street stood the gleaming white limo, long as a yacht. And there was Ginger, shooting his cuffs and making sure he could be seen by whatever poor fools still happened to be on the street at that hour.

Beverly didn't waste any time. 'Ginger, you promised to get us out of this dump!'

'Hey, lighten up, Bev honey. I'm workin' on it.' Ginger's voice could trip a lie detector over the phone. 'We gotta find the perfect spot. The ideal venue. This is a delicate matter. I'm trying to mould a career for you ladies –'

'Only career we have is starvin' to death,' Ronette snorted.

'– I mean, I'm not some funky job-droid, you know. I know you girls are artists. But I'm an artist, too.' Ginger smiled at Beverly. 'You're the leader, Bev. You know what I mean.' He leaned in close. Beverly tried to hide her disgust, but not all that hard. 'I sense a chemistry of leadership between us, Bev. I think we should talk about it.'

She wanted to pull back – and maybe slug him in the chops, for good measure – but instead she held her ground. 'You were supposed to get us some money tonight, Ginger.'

'Hey, ladies –' He held his hands up, palm out, the aggrieved victim. 'What can I do? I tried. But the guy just bought the club. He's got cash flow problems.' He smiled at Bev again and oiled, 'You're a business woman. You know what that means.'

'That means you didn't try hard enough,' Caldonia said.

Ginger gave her a look and nodded to his driver, who leaped out and opened the rear door. The interior was a snowy landscape of white leather. 'Things are tough all over,' he said, not smiling. He climbed into the car and the driver, shouldering the women out of the way, closed the door with an expensive *pok*! Ginger smiled as the power window lowered silently. 'Anyway, he promised me next week you'll see some bread.'

'If we don't, Ginger,' Beverly said, 'we're walking.'

The smile went away. 'You may be walking, girl, but you won't be singing. Dig? Not without me. We have a contract.'

'Then you live up to it!' Ronette snapped.

Ginger glared at her for a second, then recovered his customary manner of sliminess swathed in sleaze. He looked at Beverly and said, 'Tell your friend to learn some manners. Remind her that I own you guys.' He reached out and squeezed Beverly's hand. 'Be happy, babe.' He nodded to the driver and the mammoth car glided off, one red indicator winking as it got away. Just like Ginger.

'Now, normally I don't approve of murder,' K.C. said dryly. 'But I'm thinking about making an exception.'

Still looking in the direction of the car, Beverly said, 'Two more months. Two months and that's it.'

'Two months?' Ronette laughed. 'You heard him. We got a contract. Probably expires like in 1999.'

Bev looked at her gravely. 'I mean me. Two more months of this rock 'n' roll frustration and then that's it. Adios amigos.'

'Yeah, and buenos dias what?' Ronette said. 'You gonna earn big money in computer programming? Gonna learn to drive the big rigs? Face it, honey; you can sing, and you can play, but otherwise it's all waitin' tables. And there's too many actresses out there even to get those jobs.'

K.C. yawned and shrugged. 'Well, maybe we'll get lucky, and old Ginger'll drive over a cliff. You want a ride home, Bev?'

Beverly shook her head. 'I'm gonna try to walk this off. If I get home too soon I'll just stomp around being mad.' She started to walk towards the alley at the side of the club. 'See you guys tomorrow.'

'Be careful,' Caldonia said. 'In this neighbourhood it's

weirdo time in about ten minutes.'

'I will. See ya.'

The others headed off towards their cars as Bev walked glumly around the corner into the alley. Ronette was right. All Bev could really do well was sing and play. And it wasn't even a matter of finding different musicians. She loved these girls and the four of them really cooked. If Bev wasn't going anywhere with music, it's because it wasn't meant to be. She was doomed to the one thing she swore she'd avoid: an ordinary life.

She had made that resolution at the age of twelve, in sixth grade.

Beverly had been reading *Seventeen* surreptitiously, the magazine half in her lap and half in her desk, stealing glances down instead of following a passage in her social studies text book about Vasco da Gama or Rocky Balboa or one of those other explorers. While everyone else was struggling with pronouncing 'circum-navigating,' Beverly was daydreaming: she was making a sweeping, drop-dead entrance into a swirling, pounding disco. The music thumped and churned like a relentless machine. Everybody was smoking cigarettes and drinking beer without getting into trouble. The revellers spun and bobbed, circum-navigating the strobe-dazzled dance floor in heady abandon – until they beheld her.

She was clad in luscious gold lamé and do-it-to-me high heels, her makeup flawless, her companion hunk-like, her driver's licence in her very own sequined clutch bag, her eyes like rare jewels, capable of mesmerizing anyone – men, women, children, even dogs (it hardly mattered) – that they happened to grace with a provocative glance . . .

'Beverly, are you with us?' her teacher asked.

'Um . . .' She'd flushed, shoved the magazine into her desk, and desperately scanned the text book for the answer to a question that had not been asked. 'Sir Francis Drake?'

'What?'

'What?'

'Sir Francis Drake what, Beverly?'

'Um . . . uh . . .'

The teacher had walked over and motioned silently with a wave of her hand: give it over. Bev reached in, burning purple in embarrassment, which is to adolescents as malaria is to the rest of the human race. She produced the contraband publication and watched it disappear into the custody of the authorities. Titters and whispers flitted through the class, especially from the hated Jeanette Horvath, whom Beverly took great pride in despising ever since an incident two years before – some playground outrage involving beanbags.

The teacher glanced in cold disapproval at the magazine and said, 'Please pay attention to what the group is doing. You're no different from anyone else, you know.'

A yelp of triumphant glee went up from Jeanette Horvath (Bev couldn't see her but she just knew), and in that moment one teenage girl's life-theme was set. 'I am,' she heard herself say. Probably she merely meant, 'I may be like a lot of these kids, but I sure as hell am not like that stupid Jeanette Horvath,' but the operatic grandeur of what she actually did say impressed her. It didn't impress the teacher, who snorted, 'In this classroom, you are not,' but no matter; from that day to this, Beverly Switzler's main (and sometimes only) definition of herself, which had begun in the form of her not being Jeanette Horvath, had matured into the notion that she was not ordinary.

Then why were things such a drag?

Maybe it was Cleveland. Nothing ever happened there. Call it a fact of life, or geography, or luck, but the exciting things and the interesting people just happened to be somewhere else – L.A. and New York mainly. And it was a self-perpetuating process; when everybody who was anybody lived on one coast or another, anybody who was somebody went there. In which case, how could anything happen to anybody in dumb old Cleveland? It would take a man from Mars, dropping down out of the sky, to drum up some excitement here . . .

Beverly was a tough, self-sufficient young lady who didn't believe in feeling sorry for herself. And the heartless (and often mindless) world of garage bands and diveroo night clubs was an environment particularly hostile to self-pity. But she had just put out a ton of energy on a five-hour gig, and had got back zero. So she was uncharacteristically mopey, and for that reason just didn't see the two surly punk-types hanging out against the scorched brick wall halfway down the alley.

They saw her, though.

'Hey, righteous lady,' one said. He had a complexion compared to which the moon looked like Kim Alexis, the Grand Canyon like Barbara Alexis, and an anchovy pizza like 'Aunt' Nancy. 'Loved your sounds, man.'

Bev looked up and started. 'Oh – thanks.' She forced a smile, made a fast bit of token eye contact, and went into her fend-off-the-maniacs stride. 'Well, gotta go. Bye now.'

The other one stepped forward. He wore a studded leather jacket and was bald. He reminded her of the wild-eyed goon in *The Road Warrior* – the one who chained himself to the front of the jeep for the climactic battle – except he lacked that guy's charm. 'Could I, like, have your autograph?'

This was threatening to turn bad. Beverly hesitated, and said, 'Um, well, where . . .? I don't –'

'How 'bout on my shirt,' the skinhead said. Then he did the one thing she hoped he wouldn't do. He laughed.

It was the high-pitched, revved-up giggle of a creep looking for trouble and willing, if he couldn't find any, to invent some. Bev said, 'Sorry. Catch ya later.'

She started to hustle past them, but they fell in step on either side.

'Yeah, me, too,' Moonface said. 'I want you to autograph my shorts.'

The bald guy giggled. 'Then you can sign my head.'

Increasing her speed, Bev said, 'Look, not tonight, guys, okay? Just cool it –'

The skinhead grabbed her upper arm and slammed her into a line of trash cans against a building. 'Hey, we're talking to you, big rock star!' There was a gigantic crash of galvanized metal against brick. He had her pinned against the damp, cold wall. 'Who do you think you are, babe?'

Howard the Duck had been dreaming. Nothing special – one of those typical semi-nonsensical dreams.

He was walking down DeCoy Avenue on his way to buy tickets for the Superbill. Then all of a sudden he found himself in a supermarket, wandering down an endless aisle of canned goods. For some reason he felt a compelling need to buy a can of corn, but when he arrived at the proper shelf, it was bare – except for one gigantic, empty can. Then – this is how crazy dreams are – he found himself actually climbing into the can! The last thing Howard saw, before his vision was obscured by its rim, was of one of the stockboys running up the aisle towards him. The stockboy must have objected to Howard's being in the can though, because he evidently started banging on its side, and banging and banging, louder and louder and –

Howard woke with a jolt. It all came back to him: the flying chair, the menacing mutants, SATAN'S SLAVES, 'geek,' Mama, Billy, 'Yuck,' everything. Now he was in a garbage can that smelled like several things in addition to corn. Someone or something had knocked the lid off. A tussle was going on above.

'Let me go, you vicious creep!'

'Hey,' laughed a lazy, mean voice. 'Don't go snot-nosed on us, sweets. We're your biggest fans.'

Howard looked up. Two more of those leather-clad soldiers, or police, or whatever they were, were molesting a female. She looked familiar . . .

She said, 'Yeah, right – !' and brought her knee up into the crotch of the one with the unhealthy-looking face. He went 'Oooofff!' and sank from view. The other man, his head as bald as the egg from which Howard had been hatched, grabbed the woman's arm and twisted it, then forced her towards the ground.

'Let me go! Help!'

This was no dream. Howard had only been on this planet a few hours, but even he recognized a female in distress when he saw one. It really burned his tail feathers. He hated bullies. He'd hated them ever since fourth grade, when a duckling in his class had roughed him up during recess and called him 'mallardjusted'.

'Somebody! HELP!'

'That does it,' Howard thought. 'No more Mr Nice Duck!' Gathering the full fury of his duck-wrath into a ferocious little bundle, he uncoiled in a leap, sprang up out of the can and yelled, 'EeeaaaaAAAAAHHHHH!'

The two punks who had been wrestling Beverly to the ground stopped dead. So did Bev. In fact all three of them more or less froze in position, half on their feet and half on their knees, a tableau for which 'Punks Molesting Young Woman' would not have been a bad title. All three were struck dumb by the sight of . . . well, of this three-foot duck, jumping up out of one trash can onto the top of the one beside it and pointing a, um, finger (do ducks have fingers?) at them.

'LET THE FEMALE GO!' thundered the unusual bird.

The skinhead managed, 'Huh?'

'I've had it!' The duck spoke English, which was ridiculous. 'I've been shot through space and banged around this alley and dragged into buildings and thrown out on the street. I've been run down by trucks and beaten to death by total strangers.' The duck started talking to himself as much as to them. 'At first I figured, okay. I'm new here. Maybe this is how they do things on this planet. I'll get used to it.' He looked at them and pointed again. 'But this!

Every duck has his limit! And this is mine!'

Howard glared at the two men. It felt good – damn good – to blow off some steam. He felt as though the strength of a hundred ducks were his on command. The woman was looking at him gratefully. He was a hero –

The two goons laughed. 'Shoo!' The bald one waved his hands. 'Beat it! Like fly away!'

That did it. 'NO ONE LAUGHS AT THE MASTER OF QUACK FU!' Howard leaped. 'HIIIYYAAAAH –!'

It was sheer bluff. He had no idea what he was doing. Oh, he had taken a few classes, and still remembered a few moves and the Quack Fu Shout of Supreme Unleashing. But he'd quit after four classes – the whole thing had been too violent and mystical for him.

Nonetheless, the jump carried him onto the bouncy cushion of an abandoned car seat and up! Up! Up! He tucked into a nifty little somersault and crashed, feet-first, into the man with the horrible face. The punk went sprawling.

Howard was on the ground now, and spied a rusty iron rod nearby. He grabbed it and swung, just as the eggheaded guy reached him. The rod met its mark, somewhere near the knees. The skinhead toppled.

The other guy had recovered enough to mutter something not nice. He charged. Howard didn't see it. Beverly did – she stuck out a leg and sent him careering into the cans with a terrible clatter. Howard seized two garbage lids and, like his second cousin, a percussionist with the Fowlharmonic, brought them together around the punk's head with a mighty KHWHANNGGGG!

'Get him out of here,' Howard told the man with the egg-smooth head, jerking a thumb towards his reeling compatriot. 'Before I get mad.'

'Sure! You got it!'

One, limping, dragged the other, unconscious, out of the alley. Egghead and Moonface; together again for the last time.

Howard the Duck sighed. Victory had made him contemplative. 'This is obviously no place for a halfway intelligent, sensitive duck.'

Beverly, meanwhile, stared. The speaking bird had rendered her boggled of mind. 'You . . . you're . . . um . . .' There didn't seem to be any other way to put this. 'Are you . . . like, really a . . . duck?'

('This trip has been murder on my self-esteem,' Howard thought.) 'Yeah, I'm a duck,' he said. 'Any more questions?'

'Huh?' She hadn't expected him to be so forthright. 'Are you okay?'

'Fine. Peachy.'

Beverly found herself babbling as the tension of the past few minutes eased. 'You were great. That jump was amazing. I mean I want to thank you for helping me –'

'Now do I get to ask a question?' Howard looked around. 'Where the heck am I?'

She pointed towards the far end of the alley. 'That's Powell over there, and a block down is Ninth, where the light is –'

'I mean what is this place? What's it called?'

'You mean . . . Cleveland . . .?'

Howard snorted. 'Cleveland. Land of Cleves. Perfect name for this planet –'

'No, Cleveland's the name of the city.' She started to laugh. Imagine, confusing the name of a city with . . . 'You mean what planet?' Bev began to back away. Talking ducks were one thing. They were interesting as a phenomenon. Most definitely out of the ordinary. But talking ducks from other planets were just too weird. A person had to have limits. 'It's called Earth. I think. Ha ha. Wow. So, anyway, nice meeting you, and, thanks, and, uh, have a nice day . . .'

Beverly began to hustle out of there. She would have made it, too, had not a sudden detonation of thunder signalled the arrival of the storm the weatherman had been promising for three days. Instinctively she turned – and beheld a really rather endearing three-foot duck, standing alone in the god-

35

forsaken alley, raising the collar of his satin jacket against the first fat raindrops and extracting a stubby cigar from an inner pocket. She had been hoping for a man from Mars; instead she'd got a duck with a stogie. It would have to do.

'Have you got someplace to go?' she asked.

He zipped up his jacket. 'Lady, if I had someplace to go,' he said, jamming the cigar in his bill, 'I sure wouldn't be in Cleveland.'

A duck after her own heart.

Four

They walked for about fifteen minutes through the deserted streets of the Earth city known as Cleveland. Naturally Howard didn't mind the rain – it rolled off him like etc. – but apparently it made these creatures uncomfortable. The woman walked faster as it fell harder. Since Howard's stride was much shorter than hers, he had to run.

That was okay, too. It was a pleasure to be out of that alley. The air was cleaner, and the wind that had brought in the storm was fresh and bracing. Out from under those grimy buildings at last, he could see the immense, black sky overhead. Somewhere, up there, was Duck World. Just seeing the heavens made him feel a little less trapped. Now and then a car hissed by, its lights revealing the slanting raindrops. The buildings, the houses, the shops, the cars – everything reminded him of his native planet, except that here everything was on a slightly larger scale, and the dominant species was essentially non-duck.

They came to a warehouse-like building, as long as the block and faced with big industrial windows. 'Here's where I live,' she said. After trudging up two flights of steps ill-suited to Howard's short legs, they came to a windowless metal door bristling with locks. She fished and fumbled with ten thousand keys until it opened, and she let him into a dark room. She flipped a switch on the wall.

Howard beheld a large open space cluttered with clothes, guitars, furniture, magazines, sheet music, pencils, cassettes, records. Cans of beer and soda could be seen. There was a visible presence of pink doughnut boxes. The area was not unlittered with greasy transparent bags of fried snack foods. Various indefinable undergarments – satiny, filmy things in frightening shapes, of uncertain function – greeted the unwary, uncomprehending, faintly grossed-out duck's eye. He was not particularly fastidious, but this was a little appalling.

'Sorry about the place,' the woman said. She began scurrying about, picking up clothes and records, shoving them into drawers or boxes, stowing bags of cookies in cabinets. She slowed down only to lift, with reverence and care, an acoustic guitar, gently returning it to its velvet-lined, coffin-like case. Howard watched, fascinated. 'It's a sort of disaster area these days,' she went on. 'We're working on some new songs, and what happens is the girls come over and hang out all day –'

The girls hang out? In Howard's imagination arose an image of young ladies draped over the window sills, as though drying in the sun. Assuming this planet got sun. Maybe it rained all the time. Something else to worry about. 'Who? What?'

'The group. Cherry Bomb. It's this band I'm in –'

That was where he'd seen her before. 'At that club tonight?' he asked. 'I saw you up on stage.'

'Some pit, huh?' She was still flitting around, perhaps a little nervous at the presence of this three-foot waterfowl. 'But what can we do?' she went on anxiously, bunching up an old shirt and shoving it in the refrigerator. 'Until we get our big break, we're stuck. I mean, we have this manager, but he's a total jerk –' She stopped and looked at him. 'I'm sorry. You probably don't have any idea what I'm talking about, do you, Mr . . . um . . . Mr Duck . . .'

'It's Howard.'

She looked puzzled. 'What is?'

'My name.'

'Really? Like literally Howard?'

'Like literally.' He scowled. 'What's wrong with that?'

'Nothing!' She seemed to blush a little, and laughed. 'I mean, this whole thing is so weird, man, right? I mean, first you're this giant duck, and then your name is, like, Howard –'

She was babbling, possibly to keep from fainting. 'So it's, like, "Hey, I'd like you to meet Howard, he's this—" '

'Please.' He held up a hand. Suddenly he was the one about to faint. Again. 'If you think it's weird for you, think how I feel. I'm the one who's out of his element here.'

She nodded quickly. 'Oh, right. Sorry. Okay. My name's Beverly. Beverly Switzler. Can I get you something to eat? Ducks eat, right? I have some milk. I can put it in a bowl or something.'

Howard took a few steps, idly inspecting the place and hoping his irritation didn't show. At least, not too much. 'Doll, I don't drink milk out of bowls,' he said. 'Frankly, I could use a brew right about now.'

'A broo.' She pondered. It was her first contact with an alien language. How strange it was! How unpronounceable by a regular human mouth! This was exciting. 'I don't know if we have "broo" on . . . you know . . . on Earth—'

'A beer. Got a beer handy?'

'Oh — a beer! Right. Sure.' She spun towards the refrigerator and flung open the door. 'God, who put this in here?' She pulled out the crumpled shirt and threw it on a chair. 'I'm sorry I'm so nervous,' she went on, popping the can. 'I haven't been around animals that much. I mean I never had a pet or anything . . .' She joined him in the living space of the loft and handed him the can. 'I mean, it always seemed like such a hassle, right? Always feeding them, cleaning up their little poo-poos—'

'I'll try to control myself,' Howard said.

'Oh, hey, no offence. I mean I can see you're an adult, so you're probably . . . you know . . .'

He took a slug of the beer and said, 'Housebroken?'

She sighed. 'I'm sorry. I'm really blowing this, aren't I? Anyway, why don't you sit down and make yourself at home . . .'

'I wish,' Howard said, and eased himself down onto a faded easy chair from which the stuffing had begun a slow but inexorable escape. The beer wasn't bad – on the lighter side, like Birdweiser back home – and the chair was soft. Nothing like a night of unmitigated terror to make you appreciate the little things . . .

What happened next was . . . well, what happened next was, the chair started to move: There was a slight but palpable vibration and its feet did a little chattering flamenco on the floor. Howard froze, yelled, 'OH NO!' and leapt up. The chair fell over backwards. He found himself tumbling against a wall. He caught a glimpse of Beverly, wide-eyed, backing up in fright against a bookcase –

Then, for a second, he was once more on his own chair, crashing through his apartment wall, past Herb and Edna, out into the night sky and off into space. He was riveted in place, shooting through the void, helpless –

'Howard?' Beverly was leaning over him. 'Are you all right?'

'The chair started to move!' he said.

To his shock, she simply shrugged. 'Happens all the time. Whenever some big truck goes by outside.'

'Some big truck –!' He sighed and came to his feet. 'Listen, Beverly, you have to understand. One minute I'm just sitting in my living room, and the next minute I'm flying across the universe!'

She nodded. 'What a drag. Really.'

'My whole world is gone!' He began to pace. The enormity of what had happened was finally sinking in. 'What the hell am I doing here? You're a featherless biped – and I'm a duck! This is all wrong!'

'That's not nice.'

He stopped and looked at her. 'What?'

'Calling me . . . that. I know you've been through a lot, and I'm sorry, but –'

'Beverly, that's the kind of creature you are. All of us. My world is all ducks and yours is two-legged creatures without feathers. At least that's the only kind of creature

40

I've see so far. Are there any others?'

She shrugged. 'A lot of people have cats. But basically we're the ones in charge.'

'Right. So look at how out of place I am.' He retrieved the beer from the floor. Most of it was still in the can. He took a sip. 'Talk about an identity crisis. Suppose you suddenly found yourself on an entire planet of ducks!'

'Oh, God,' she said, 'I'd probably totally flip out.'

'Exactly.'

'You mean you're really, like, an average citizen of your planet?' The evenhanded reasonableness of this exchange made her nervous, seemed out of keeping with the essential weirdness of the situation. 'You're not, like, some emissary of a higher intelligence –'

'Me?'

'– bringing world peace to mankind? You don't have some warning from the Galactic Guardians to stop being an immature civilization, or something?'

He went to the window and pointed towards the sky. 'I'M AN AVERAGE DUCK FROM DUCK WORLD! Sorry. Didn't mean to shout. Believe me, I'm just a regular bird. I have a job, and an apartment –'

'What do you do? Go to school?'

'Well . . .' he shrugged. It was a touchy subject. 'I went to med. school once.'

'Oh, yeah? To be a vet?'

He looked at her. 'To be a doctor.' When she grimaced, he went on, 'It was my parents' idea.' Howard sounded apologetic. 'They used to make me watch re-runs of *Marcus Webfeet M.D.* They thought it would be nice if I became a plastic surgeon – you know, make the big dough doing beak jobs and tail tucks.'

'Uh-huh . . .'

Beverly very carefully went to the refrigerator for a drink. Things were not becoming less strange – on the contrary. All she found on the shelves were beer and a bottle of

41

champagne. But it wasn't champagne. It was cold duck. She took the beer. 'What happened?'

'I dropped out,' Howard the Duck said. 'Decided to find out about real life. On the streets. So I became a folk singer for awhile, then wrote poetry at night and did construction work by day.'

'That sounds great –'

He shrugged. 'Nobody else thought so. Everybody kept telling me to grow up, grow up . . . I figured they must know something I didn't. So I bagged the whole thing and got a straight job last month.'

'Doing what?'

'Advertising.'

She looked at him closely. 'Really . . .?'

'Copy writer. Actually it's sort of creative, really. They used my line for the Diane von Furstenbird account. Her new perfume. "Flapper. Because all's fowl in love . . . and war." '

Beverly said, not meeting his eyes, 'I don't know, Howard. Sounds to me like you sort of sold out.'

'Yeah, well so did half my generation.' He grew brisk. Beverly sensed that this was something he'd thought about a good deal, but wasn't eager to discuss. 'Spent their twenties squawking about the power structure, and their thirties kissing its . . . tail.'

'Are you *that* old?'

'Yeah.' He shrugged. 'I used to think there was some kind of special destiny out there, waiting for me. Now . . .' He looked away. 'All I want is to be left alone.'

'Man,' she said, and gulped her beer. 'That sounds grim. What about the rest of the world?'

'What about it?' He tapped some cigar ash into a Cleveland Indians ashtray. 'Why should I care about it when nobody else does?'

' 'Cause if you don't, you're just like them.'

'Fine. Which means I'll make a living and stay out of

trouble. Besides, I don't exactly see how one duck can make any difference. Especially if he's me . . .' He took a puff. 'Nope, all I want is to get back home, and put everything back the way it was –'

Beverly snapped her fingers. 'Howard – maybe that special destiny is why you're here! I mean, they say there're no accidents in the universe . . . and you sure can't explain your coming here in any normal way. Maybe you can't stay out of trouble. Maybe you've been brought here . . . for some greater cosmic cause!'

'Then I wish whoever did it would get on with it,' Howard said, disgusted. 'Because I have no intention of waiting around for some cosmic cause. I have to get back home, period!'

('An alien creature on Earth, wanting to get home . . .' Beverly thought. 'Where have I heard that before . . .?') She shook her head, contemplating the problem of returning a duck to his native planet. Walking around the loft, she thought out loud. 'We have to get some kind of help. Like the authorities, or somebody. NASA, maybe. But what do we do? Call up Information and say, "Hi, gimme NASA, I want to send a duck into outer space . . .?"'

She looked at her visitor and discovered that he had fallen asleep, on his broad, webbed feet, head leaning against the windowpane. She approached cautiously. 'Howard . . .?' He didn't stir. Beverly sighed, relieved. The poor bird – he'd been through a lot. Carefully, she reached out her hand and touched him. His feathers felt like . . . feathers. He really was a duck. Meanwhile Howard settled onto the window seat, still snoozing. It didn't look too comfortable.

Carefully, holding her breath, Beverly grasped him in both hands and lifted him like a sleeping child. He was surprisingly light. Her guitar weighed more. She carried him over to the lumpy, threadbare couch and gently laid him down. The whole time she did this, she waited for herself to wake up, or come down off of whatever bizarre drug someone had slipped her at the club when she wasn't looking. But Howard the Duck kept being there, kept sleeping on her couch, kept feeling like a gently snoozing package of down. Bev herself felt completely normal.

She was forced to conclude that all this was real. She went over to her bed and got a pillow and a blanket, then slipped the one under and the other on top of the recumbent fowl. He tossed a little but remained asleep. Her foot hit something on the floor. It must have fallen when she moved him: his wallet.

Beverly made it a point of honour never to snoop in her dates' personal accessories, but this struck her as being a reasonable exception. Inside Howard's wallet she found what must have been the usual items for a duck of Howard's socio-economic background: a driver's licence with his picture, an American Eggspress card, some money, a photo of Howard with two older ducks who must be his parents . . . even a little snapshot of Howard at the beach, in bathing suit and cigar, flanked by two sexy little ducklets.

Her throat swelled, and some tears welled up. She gently put the wallet back into his pocket. He slept on.

Bev went into the kitchen area. She had no idea what to do next. Whom should she call? Immigration? She grabbed the phone book and started flipping through the Yellow Pages, looking for inspiration. Pet hotels? Pet Finders –?

'Vets!' she whispered. But Howard didn't really need a doctor . . . 'Oh, what the hell, it's a start –'

The phone rang. She grabbed it and whispered, 'Hello?'

'Hi, kid.' It was Ronette. Beverly could hear music and voices in the background – probably K.C. and Caldonia were there with her. 'Listen, we decided what we need is a big hotshot lawyer, get us out of that damn contract with Ginger.'

Beverly felt the whole problem with Ginger and the band slide back onto her like a load of stone from a dump truck. 'Yeah, fine,' she said. 'And how we gonna pay this big hotshot lawyer? Free cassettes? Gonna take it out in trade?'

'Bite your tongue, girl.' Ronette sounded aggrieved, not wanting to be brought down by trifles. 'I don't know – deferred contingency, or whatever they call it. We get rid of Ginger, get some real gigs, and –'

'Ronnie, listen, I can't talk about it now. Something really intense has happened –'

'Why're you whispering? You got somebody over there? One of your pitiful dates?'

'Uh . . . sort of. Hey,' Beverly said, seizing on an idea. 'Speaking of pitiful dates, remember that scientist guy you went out with last summer? The big brain? What was his name?'

'Who, that lame? His name was Phil Blumburtt. Why do you want to call him? I told you all about that . . . the date which will live in infamy . . .'

Bev said, 'Didn't he work with animals?'

'Yeah.' Ronette laughed. 'He's great with 'em – as long as they've been dead for thirty millions years. He's a palaeontologist. That means fossils, kid. You want him to fix you up with an older man?'

'What's his number?'

Ronette told her and Beverly hung up. It was true that Howard wasn't exactly a fossil. But he wasn't exactly business as usual, either. How could any animal scientist not be interested in a three-foot talking duck from another planet?

As she dialled his number Bev realized that, while she should have been exhausted, she felt just fine. Things were becoming less ordinary.

Five

How glorious was the following day! Overnight the rain washed the great metropolis of Cleveland like some kind of giant shower, flushing its thoroughfares, rinsing its stupid cars, and filling its reservoirs with life-sustaining water. Then, having courteously expended itself before dawn, the storm dissipated, leaving behind a cloudless sky in which the sun might rise in a majestic, golden manner.

How perfect a day for being up and about! Quick – what shall one do? Trot off to work? Scamper off to school? Straighten up the house? Enjoy healthy exercise out of doors? Shop for quality consumer items in one of the city's many fine local commercial establishments?

Beverly Switzler would have none of that kind of thing. Her chief activity, this beautiful morning, concerned her house guest, who was a duck. He wore a string tie and a satin jacket. He smoked cigars – Quackanudos, usually – and he spoke English. It was a phenomenon. So naturally Beverly shoved him into a big trash bag and loaded him into a cab for a ride to the museum.

'This is humiliatin',' Howard snarled. He could barely see out of the two eye-holes she had gouged in the dark green plastic. The bag was secured over his head, his feet resting on the bottom. He couldn't walk. He had to be carried.

'I'm sorry, Howard,' Beverly said. 'But I don't want people freaking out all over the place when they see you.' She imitated a gawking passerby. '"O wow, man, like what a awesome duck. He must be some kind of nucular mutation."' She shook her head. 'I could get arrested for harbouring an illegal alien.'

'This is your idea of a solution?' He slapped at the inside of

46

the bag. 'I'll be talking about this to some shrink for the rest of my life!'

'Don't be such a crybaby. We're almost there.'

The cab driver, keeping his eyes scrupulously on the road, managed to lean back towards Beverly and said, 'I see ya got one of them computer-chip talking dolls. I tell ya it's amazin' what they can do with stuff these days.'

'Shut up,' Howard said from inside the bag.

The cabbie chuckled. 'I love it.'

The Museum of Natural History was one of those elaborately decorated Beaux Arts-style, hyper-gussied-up wedding-cake buildings that made you feel intimidated and inadequate just looking at it. No matter how interesting the exhibits inside, two steps over the threshold and you were exhausted, half-suffocated, and vaguely depressed. Beverly, however, was too busy to succumb to its effect this time. She had an appointment with a scientist about a sackful of duck. She paid the cabbie while Howard squirmed and snorted in the bag on the pavement.

'I gotta get my kid one of them,' the hack said, finding change. 'Whattaya call it?'

'None of your business,' Howard squawked from inside.

'It's called Howard,' Beverly said nervously.

'Mind if I take a look?'

'Well . . .' Quickly, she flashed open the top. The cabbie leaned across the front seat and peered inside. Howard glared back and said, 'Do you mind?' Beverly shut the bag.

The cabbie looked puzzled. 'What is that, one of them dodo birds?'

'It's a duck.'

'Howard, huh. Great name.' He nodded, impressed. 'Clever item.' He drove off.

'I need this,' Howard said as Beverly carried him up the steps to the museum. 'I haven't been degraded enough on this planet. Now I'm a clever item.'

'He was just being nice,' she whispered, hoping no one saw her talking to the bag.

'Yeah – ow! Take it easy!'

'Sorry.' She had put him down and was now dragging the bag down the hall. 'You get heavy after a while.'

'Then lemme walk!'

'Shush.'

The crisp, over-precise directions of a passing scientist led her to the research wing, where she found Phil Blumburtt's laboratory door. She knocked. Blumburtt answered.

Beverly remembered him from his date with Ronette; in his mid-twenties, cutish, but nothing to write home about and with a hyped-up, high-energy personality Beverly wasn't sure whether she found appealing or irritating. She always felt a little insecure around intellectual types, but Phil was so revved-up and intense he wasn't all that different from a few drummers she knew.

He let her in. The door, on its hallway side, could be seen to close and remain shut. Several people passed it in the course of their daily activities: a secretary walked by, carrying several folders. An archaeologist and a geologist crossed its section of hall, talking animatedly about a valley in Africa. A security guard strolled past on his normal rounds.

Then the door flew open and Phil Blumburtt 'exploded' out of the room. He raced down the hallway like a complete maniac. The tail of his white lab coat fluttered and snapped as he turned a corner. He ran down another hall, then barged into a large workroom where a team of bone men were assembling the skeleton of what was probably the most significant ichthyosaur find in two decades. They looked up.

'MY GOD!' Blumburtt shouted. He was panting, pacing, possessed. Think of Captain Kirk, having a fit about some crisis of command, but without the arbitrary pauses, meant to seem spontaneous, for effect. The intensity. The at-stakeness of things. 'I've seen it! I've – this is it! Right here! Some woman! BAM! Right out of the bag! I said, Well, well, what have we h – And then! Hello? It's – well, I mean, for one thing – it's unbelievable! It's –!'

Then, abruptly, he stopped, and shut the hell up. Phil Blumburtt, despite appearances, was not stupid. He paused. A certain understandable amount of self-interested calculation took place in his heart and mind. He did not experience a crisis of command. Instead, he smiled, and waved a little wave of unimportance.

'It's nothing,' he said, shuffling towards the door. 'Never mind. Nice bones. Admire your work. Everybody.' As he left he shut the door with the elaborate delicacy of a blabbermouth trying to rein in a big secret.

The bone men shrugged and turned back to the skeleton. One said, 'Looks like Blumburtt forgot to take his sanity pill today,' and they all had a damn good laugh.

Meanwhile, in the hallway, Blumburtt strode like a total lunatic back to his office, whispering frantically to himself and discovering that he was in perfect agreement with everything he said. 'Why should I tell them?' he said. 'Why should I get them involved? Why should I let the museum take credit? After all, it's *my* discovery!'

COVERAGE-IN-DEPTH INSERT 2
Phil Blumburtt: *Why I Wear What I Wear*

Philip Geoffrey Blumburtt (B.S., M.S., University of Miami at Ohio of Montana at Cleveland in Ohio near Chicago of Illinois) feels that science plays an important part in the nation's life. As one of his generation's top palaeontologists, he feels keenly his responsibility both to advance his career and keep his wardrobe looking good – while at the same time dressing in a way that shows respect for the creatures whose remains he studies.

'I have this fantasy of taking a time machine back to the Jurassic,' he notes wryly. 'I'd like to visit all the animals I've studied when they were alive. Then I'd want to be able to look them in the face and hear them tell me, "Hey – Phil, you're okay."' He adds, 'That's where proper grooming fits in.'

When not dressing to impress ten-million-year-old mastodons, Phil Blumburtt spends his time dressing to impress his wardrobe. He favours a traditional look: conservative, trim, conveying a timeless sense of quiet stylishness. Slacks play a big part – Blumburtt refuses to be seen in public without trousers – as do shoes. 'Ever try walking these stone-covered museum floors barefoot? Forget it.'

Of course, there's always a place for the occasional touch of rakish detail. In Blumburtt's case that means shoelaces which, while themselves matching each other, may – or may not – be the same colour as his socks. 'I believe in letting my personal charisma speak for itself,' he asserts. 'I don't need to blow my own horn – or anybody else's, either. The only horn I need to blow is . . . I mean, I don't go around blowing horns.'

When not not going around blowing horns, Phil spends his time not blowing his image as one of America's top young anthropologists. 'Without science, we'd have no way to take our temperature,' he notes. 'Then we'd get sick, and how would we get to the hospital, which wouldn't exist?'

Later, when the day's concerns of palaeontology and anthropology yield to the more social side of life, Phil slips into the kind of formal-but-casual evening wear favoured by men and women exactly like him. 'I don't think it's unscientific to have "fun," ' he admits. 'And I dress accordingly. I favour shirts that fit my particular body.'

Evenings may find him frequenting one of several favourite cafés or restaurants or cafeterias or mini-markets, or slipping a bag of fast-food hamburgers and french fried potatoes under his arm for enjoying at home. 'I like to watch *MacNeil/Lehrer* while I eat,' notes this man of many interests.

His wardrobe for such at-home relaxation? 'Pretty much what I wear to work, plus a napkin. Is that okay?'

As for there being a woman in his life, Blumburtt is maddeningly coy about the subject. He does, however, admit to knowing 'a couple of girls,' one of whom is a certain Ronette of the local girl-group Cherry Bomb. 'We dig each other,' he comments. 'I have an affinity for rock 'n' roll. It's like palaeontology, except they use guitars.'

Blumburtt adjusts his wardrobe to suit the moment, whether it's cruising Cleveland's hot club scene, or escaping with Ronette à deux for a quiet night of romance. He remarks, 'I take all my clothes off when we have sex, so that's my "wardrobe" for that. But then, so does everyone. Don't they? They do. Don't they? Sure. I do, anyway. I don't like keeping my clothes on for something like that. They get wrinkled.'

When not not keeping his clothes on, Blumburtt indulges in some uncharacteristically immodest self-assessment. 'My goal is to be the most famous palaeontologist in the world,' he declares. And the best dressed? 'Oh. Yeah, sure. Why not.'

Phil Blumburtt's 'discovery' stood on an examination table in his lab, glad to be out of the bag but otherwise suspicious about the featherless biped in the white coat, who now burst back in through the door and circled him with a hungry look and a manic eye.

'Absolutely fantastic,' Phil murmured, pacing around Howard and staring. 'From the vast, limitless reaches of the cosmos. Space. The final frontier.' Howard plucked a cigar from his inside pocket and lit up, puffing, as Phil continued to circle and marvel. 'For CENTURIES! The one unanswered question. ARE WE ALONE? In the . . . cosmos. How . . . inconceivable . . . another life-form . . . must . . . be . . .'

Blumburtt spun suddenly and fixed Beverly with his burning gaze. 'And when we finally make contact! What will they be like? These non-humans? Gaseous beings of incorporeal form? Plant-animal hybrids of a non-carbon-based evolution? Beings . . .' His eyes glowed. 'Beings of PURE INTELLIGENCE?' (Howard shot Beverly a look that said: This guy's nuts.) 'Without BODIES? Entities of UN-CONFINED ENERGY?'

Phil, somewhat melodramatically, laughed. 'But no.' It was not clear to whom he was speaking by this point. Perhaps he fancied himself an entity of unconfined energy. 'It is none of these.' He came up close to Howard. Howard did not make an effort to avoid blowing cigar smoke into the scientist's face. 'Our first real contact with an extraterrestrial intelligence . . . is . . . with . . . a . . . d –! He suddenly leaned towards Howard and said, loudly, as though the duck were deaf, 'Phone home? Phone home? E.T. duckie want phone home?'

Howard stared back at him, then removed his cigar with George Burnsian deliberation and said, 'I suggest you see a qualified mental health professional.'

'Phil, calm down,' Beverly said. 'You've got to help us.'

'Want little candies?' Phil said. He began slapping himself on the breast and thighs, searching his pockets for the Reese's Pieces he knew he had never tasted. He yelled at Howard, 'Want itty-bitty yum-yum candies?'

'Sure,' Howard said. 'Whattaya got?'

'Phil, you don't have to talk to him like that,' Beverly said. 'He's as smart as you are.'

'Thanks, Bev,' Howard said.

'You're right,' Phil said, abandoning his Extraterrestrial Communication Babytalk Mode. 'The being is highly intelligent. WAIT! THAT'S IT! Our first test!' He went to a cabinet against a wall and returned with an armful of objects, which he dropped with a clatter onto the table at Howard's feet. 'We are about to determine whether Howard has any abilities we humans do not have . . . any, shall we say . . . super powers . . .?' He held up a heavy iron rod for all to see.

Then, gravely, he dropped it at Howard's feet. It landed with a clank. 'Now, Howard. I want to know if you can bend that.'

Howard looked at the rod. Then he looked at the scientist and said, 'Now, Phil. I want to know if you're out of your mind.'

'Howard –' Beverly began.

'Okay,' Phil said, and held up a block of wood. 'We call this . . . "wood". Can you see through it, Howard?'

'Hey, I think I can, Phil,' Howard said.

'YOU CAN –?'

'Well, I can see what's behind it . . .'

'WHAT, HOWARD? WHAT'S BEHIND IT?'

'You are, Phil. Does that count?'

'Howard, co-operate,' Beverly said.

'Very well,' the scientist said. He held up the same block and said, 'Now I want to see if you can burn a hole in this with your X-ray vision . . . !'

Howard shook his head. 'No can do, Phil. I need my X-ray contacts for that, and I left 'em at home.'

Phil looked at the duck, then said, 'I see. All right. Now I want to know can you concentrate and read my mind . . .?'

Howard put his hands to his temples and shut his eyes. He swayed slightly. Phil looked at Beverly excitedly, as though to say, Behold. A breakthrough of unparalleled significance is imminent.

But she was looking at Howard, miffed. The duck said, 'Yes . . . I'm getting something . . . I'm getting something –'

'WHAT, HOWARD! WHAT AM I THINKING?!'

'You're thinking, "Oh, God. They know Phil Blumburtt is a fraud. They know he's a lamebrain who can barely do long division . . ." '

'That's not what I'm thinking!'

'Oh. Right. Sorry. That's what I'm thinking.'

Beverly looked angry. 'Howard –'

'Okay, okay,' the scientist said. 'One final test. Can you . . . oh, how to put it . . . are you able to see into the future?'

'Yeah,' Howard said, and he leapt down off the lab table. 'I can see myself walking out that door! In about ten seconds!'

Howard started walking.

Beverly and Phil chased him as an angry Howard the Duck strode down the hall and into a central exhibition area. He waddled indignantly beneath giant skeletons of Tyrannosaurus Rex, Triceratops, Stegosaurus, and Brontosaurus, and other animals who did get respect and who had not been subjected to a barrage of insulting questions and tests. No other humans were in sight, but Phil and Beverly knew that wouldn't last long.

'Howard, wait!' Phil pleaded, keeping pace as the indignant bird stormed through the hall. 'You can't leave!'

'Watch me,' the duck said.

'But you're my ticket to the Hall of Fame! Articles in *Scientific American*! Regular appearances on *MacNeil/Lehrer*! A twelve-part series on PBS! Why not? I can do the whole Sagan hypnotic-narration thing – "billions and billions of stars, around which billions and billions of planets –" '

'We're not here to make you famous, Phil,' Beverly said. 'Howard, maybe I made a mistake –'

'Look, hold it.' Phil managed to bring all of them to a halt. He glanced around nervously. If someone saw them – if anyone saw Howard – Phil's goose, which could still be persuaded to lay the golden egg – was cooked. 'I never bad mouth my fellow scientists. Why? Because I'm an ethical man. Hey, that's just how I'm put together. Okay. But Beverly, if you put Howard in someone else's hands, do you know what'll happen? Boom – dissection, CAT-scan, biopsy, blood samples, the works. Invasive procedures! Postmortems!'

'I feel sick,' Howard said.

'Right! So do I! That's why I'm your best hope, Howard!'

'All I want to know,' Howard said, 'is how I got here, and how to get back.'

'No problem!' Phil shouted. He lowered it back down to a whisper. 'I mean, I already have a theory.'

Howard looked at him closely. 'Like what?'

Phil held a finger up to his mouth: mum's the word. He led them into an exhibition area roped off with a sign reading CLOSED. They proceeded into a gallery displaying glass-faced dioramas of stuffed animals in re-created prehistoric settings. Spanning the entire wall was a mural depicting the evolution of man: from sea creature to amphibian, from vertebrate to mammal, from monkey to ape to homo sapiens.

Phil gestured expertly. 'This is how our world evolved, Howard. Life began as primal slime, and ended as . . . well, me, for example.'

'In other words, there's been absolutely no change,' Howard said. Then he actually noticed the mural. 'Wait a minute – you mean you all descended from monkeys? You're all hairless apes! That's disgusting!'

Phil, absorbed in his own rhapsodic theorizing, ignored him. 'But now imagine an alternative evolution; what I call "Blumburtt's Ascent of Duck." ' There would be simple line animation for this segment, one figure uncoiling and re-shaping into the next. The music would be Bach.

'Howard's world is exactly like Earth – except that the dominant species was not monkey, but proto-duck! So it was Duck who climbed the evolutionary ladder! Duck who dropped wings, developed arms, grew taller, and so forth. Duck's mental capacity increases! Duck forms societies and cities! Duck invents the cigar! Until, ultimately, Duck becomes the thinking, reasoning fowl we might call Anatidae Contemporaneae – today's Modern Duck!'

Phil stopped, catching his breath. It was inconceivable to him that neither of his listeners was applauding. 'Of course,' he said dramatically, 'all this took time. Many many years. Billions and billions –'

'Mr Blumburtt, just what the hell are you doing?'

The voice came from the end of the hall, from a Dr Chapin.

Phil hastily pushed Beverly and Howard behind a caveman display with a quickly whispered, 'Don't make a sound.' He turned and faced the older man.

'Have you finished cleaning the specimen lab, Blumburtt?'

'Almost finished, Dr Chapin!'

'Well get on it. Oh, and take a mop down to Marine Life – some kid tossed his cookies all over Crustaceans of the Eastern Continental Shelf.'

'Right away, sir!'

Chapin walked off just as Howard and Beverly emerged from behind Zinjanthropus In His Natural Habitat. Phil affected a smooth professional air. 'One of my colleagues –' he began.

'Baloney,' Howard said. 'You're no scientist. You're a janitor!'

'– uh, lab assistant.'

'Great,' Beverly said.

'It's only temporary! 'Til I finish school and get my own museum!'

'Thanks for nothing,' Howard said, and stomped off. Beverly followed. Blumburtt ran after them, but was stopped by the booming voice of authority.

'Damn it, Blumburtt, I said get that mop down to Marine Life!'

'In a millisecond, Dr Chapin!' He was stymied. He could only call after the receding woman and duck, 'Don't let anyone see him, Beverly! I'll think of something! Take him to a movie! I'll call you tonight! You've got to hide him!'

The scientist-to-be had a point. There are women, for example – even in our major urban areas, such as Cleveland – who will scream when they see big ducks smoking cigars. This fact was driven home forcibly to Howard and Beverly when the elevator doors opened onto the main floor of the museum. There was a woman there who, when she saw Howard, screamed.

He didn't notice. He was still seething. 'Typical,' he muttered around his stogie. 'You go to the hospital for a doctor, and they give you an intern. You go to a museum for a scientist, and you get a janitor!'

He stomped through the lobby and out the door, Beverly keeping pace, a steadily growing swarm of museum-goers and pedestrians stopping, pointing, gasping, laughing, screaming, and whispering. Howard chomped on his Quackanudo as Beverly grew peeved.

'Don't blame me!' she said as they descended the museum steps. 'I didn't know who else to call! Why are you so mad?'

Howard made for an opening on a bench – it grew larger as everyone sitting scattered at his approach – and hopped up onto it, standing. It offered access to a nearby fountain, which he mounted in a leap. Finally, he was as tall as she.

'Listen,' he said. 'If you got blasted millions of miles through space, landed on another planet where everybody thought you were a freak, and were given an I.Q. test by some janitor, you'd be mad, too!'

'Okay,' Bev said. 'But you're not making me feel guilty. I got problems, too, you know! My whole career's falling apart!'

'Your career? What about my LIFE?' Howard inadvertently struck a heroic pose, perched on the lip of the fountain. A squad of schoolchildren drifted over, led by their good-sport-but-dull teacher. 'I'm stranded!' Howard declaimed. 'Shipwrecked!'

'Now this is what I mean,' the teacher said to her charges, mincing but perky. 'Here's a wonderful exhibit that's so life-like, you almost feel as though it's alive!'

'See?' Howard said to Beverly. 'I'm a freak! A wonderful exhibit!'

'So convincing,' the teacher marvelled, unaware that the kids were giggling and staring in wonder. 'So realistic –'

'Bug off, lady. And take the brats with you.'

'I – excuse me?'

'I said BEAT IT!'

The teacher looked shocked for a moment. Then she said, to Beverly, with a strained smile and a low voice, 'Sometimes these curators take realism too far.' She led her children away.

'Howard,' Beverly said. 'You've got to try to –'

'You too,' he said. 'Leave me alone.'

'What? I'm trying to help you –'

'I don't need your help! And I don't need your charity!'

She took a step back. He was still on the fountain. 'Okay,' she said, looking away, her throat catching. I will not let this damn duck make me cry, she told herself. 'If that's what you want, you got it.' An unauthorized tear had appeared, sliding down her left cheek. She wiped it away with an angry swipe. It was time to go. 'See ya 'round, duckie.'

'Don't shed any tears for me, sweetheart,' Howard the Duck said.

'Oh, don't sweat it, I won't. You can waddle in your own self-pity, man!'

And with most of her pride intact, Beverly turned and strode off. She'd played this scene before, with guys. It wasn't so different with a duck. Any second, now, and he'd call after her –

'Yeah?' he called after her. 'Who needs you? I don't need anybody! Which is lucky,' he added, to himself, 'since I don't have anybody . . .'

He hopped down off the fountain. This, he realized, was the first day of the rest of his duck-life. He felt peppery and ready for action. When he spied several people staring fearfully at him, he obliged by rearing back and snarling like the monster they thought he was. It worked – they ran like hell. It was all good, clean fun. But he couldn't go around scaring away these hairless apes all day.

'Gotta think about practical matters,' he said aloud. If he was going to be alone, he was allowed to talk to himself. 'Gotta get food, shelter, a job . . .' He saw several other people shrinking away from him on a bench. He asked them, 'Say, where can a duck make some bread around here?'

They leapt up and ran off, warbling in fear. He'd have to refine his information-gathering technique.

Six

Roaming the streets of mighty Cleveland, Howard cleared his mental and emotional decks for a good brisk round of morose self-pity. Not that he thought of it as that. On the contrary, he probably felt he was confronting – at long last – the bitter truth about himself. So while his heart throbbed with the poignancy of his tragic predicament, his mind coolly admired his courage at being able to face it. Slump-shouldered, slow-shuffling, eyes down, mouth taut, brow furrowed, cigar dead, hands in pockets, mind numb – and proud of it! What a guy! What a performance!

No wonder that, crossing a wide boulevard, he had to leap back at the last second to avoid being hit by a bus. Has the reader ever seen (let alone heard) a municipal bus in Cleveland, or any other city? Can the reader imagine 'not see-ing' such a behemoth bearing down on him? Appreciate, then, the depths of Howard's gloom, and the extraordinary skill with which he juggled feeling sorry for himself, con-temptuous of himself, proud of himself, and oblivious to the rest of the universe, all at the same time.

He had been used and abused – not only by the assortment of goons outside the club the previous night, but by Phil Blumburtt. He pretended to care about Howard, to offer assistance in the interest of science, but actually – oh, all right. It wasn't in the interest of science. It was in the interest of landing a prestige nature show on PBS. Still, even that naked lack of pretence was wounding and insulting. So what if Blumburtt did nothing to disguise his true motives? A punch in the bill did less damage than a knife in the back, but it still hurt. Wasn't anybody on this planet motivated by the plain old desire to help someone in distress?

Maybe Beverly was. Maybe she did mean well. But – and here Howard proved himself a master at making himself miserable – the funny thing was, when it came to her, Howard didn't think he deserved her help. He had been a failure at everything he'd tried – except at his current job, although the jury was still out on that one – and the nicer Beverly (or anyone) seemed, the less Howard felt he merited their good opinion.

But wait a minute. Who did she think she was, telling him he'd 'sold out?' He secretly thought he had, of course – but what business was it of hers? And wasn't it his life, to sell out as he pleased? But if it was, then why did he care what she thought in the first place?

Offended when bad people did him wrong, not worthy when good people behaved well; no wonder Howard snarled at innocent bystanders and waited to be run over by large motor vehicles. His once-placid soul had, over the disillusioning years, become a mess, a Rubeak's Cube whose six uniform faces had got twisted and shifted and all mixed up. It had devolved into a patternless jumble of contradictions which, for about a year now, he had been trying desperately to rearrange into some kind of order.

Has the reader ever tried to bully such a Cube into working? Let him then imagine his own botched effort – reds and yellows and abutting whites and blues, with one half of the greens among the oranges, and the other half way the hell over there – as a picture of this duck's unhappy mental/spiritual state. Is it any wonder Howard wanted (or thought he wanted) to be left alone?

Of course, even a duck can only stomp around in a funk for so long. Eventually he gets hungry. So Howard found some solace in pursuing the everyday necessities of life.

He found a Goodwill Clothing Store, where he fitted himself out in a used sports jacket, crummy old T-shirt, and wrinkled slacks. He stood before the scratched full-length mirror and inspected the result. It was just as he expected. He looked ridiculous. But on this planet of giant hairless apes, he'd been forced to shop in the Tiny Fykes department; he was lucky to find anything not covered with teddy bears, robots, or (sigh) ducks.

Besides, the clothes were cheap, and at a place like this the staff wasn't too picky. The clerk took his Duck World money without a glance. (It was, by amazing coincidence, identical to U.S. currency, except for the president's portrait. Howard's twenty spot featured a jut-jawed likeness of Mallard Fillmore.) From there Howard went to his next destination.

'The story of my life,' he thought sourly as he got off the bus. 'From Goodwill to Unemployment.'

He'd drawn stares on the bus and gasps on the street, but among the huddled masses at Unemployment no one looked twice. Everyone – clients, clerks, supervisors, security – was absorbed in the mental gymnastics and gruelling self-hypnosis necessary to pretend they were somewhere else. People in line read books or stared blankly into space. Clients filling out forms mumbled to themselves, or to the forms. Government clerks, wearing big grinning buttons on their lapels reading COURTESY IS CONTAGIOUS, snarled at clients and smirked to each other. If courtesy really was contagious, they'd managed to eliminate it as a communicable threat.

Actually Howard couldn't blame them. The lobby of the ShelDrake it wasn't. The walls were a dismal civil service mint green, the counters scarred, the windows dirty, the lights a soul-destroying fluorescent white. Into this atmosphere of unending futility walked Howard the Duck, in search of hope.

Instead they gave him two forms to fill out and directed him to a counter. The ballpoint pens, chained like convicts, didn't work. After spending fifteen minutes scratching on one after another of a succession of blank forms, shredding them mercilessly without drawing ink, he managed to

62

borrow a felt marker and, as best he could, filled out the forms. Then, after a mere forty minute wait in line, he reached the counter window 'A THROUGH H.'

The clerk was a career civil servant who took neither 'civil' nor 'servant' literally. 'Ya fill out the ten-twunny-eight, ten-twunny-nine,' he asked. He looked off to the side – it was a point of pride with him that, in sixteen years on the job, he had not once looked a client in the eyes. Therefore he did not notice that this one, among other things, was too short to be seen over the counter anyway.

Howard, on tip-toe, passed him the forms.

The clerk droned, 'Place a last employment.'

'Huh?'

'Place a last employment. Where'd ya last work?'

Howard hesitated, then said, 'Does that include on my own planet?'

The clerk nodded slightly to himself, still not looking at Howard, then leaned over to his colleague at the adjacent window. 'I win,' he said. 'I ask him, Place of last employment. He says, "Does that include on my own planet?" '

'I had that guy last month,' the other clerk said.

'No, your guy said, I don't have to work, I'm from – what was it? The moon –?'

'The second moon of Jupiter.'

'Yeah. So this week I win. Right?'

'What about that lady yesterday. I ask her, Any other source of income. She says, Yeah, I own a gold mine in Brazil.'

'Can't beat "on my own planet." '

'Okay, okay. Better send him to Coramae.'

'Right.' The clerk shifted his head until once again he was not looking at Howard. 'Room two-fourteen upstairs.'

Howard thanked the clerk for not helping him, then climbed the steps to the designated office. It was smaller than the main room downstairs, but with the identical seasick-green walls and the death-warmed-over lighting. It was presided over by a very large black woman who looked like she was capable of making God eat His peas.

'Now,' she said, staring steadily into Howard's eyes. 'You do know why you've been sent to me, don't you?'

Howard attempted to strike a humorous note. 'More of my continuing streak of bad luck?'

The woman, whose name plate read 'CORAMAE THOMAS, Special Placements', leaned forward. Her leather chair squeaked under the massive shift of weight. She said, 'You've been sent to me 'cause I am famous for finding jobs for little slackers like you. They send me all the psychos, all the misfits, all the phoneys and fakers who think they can just traipse in here, and look outlandish, and they're not gonna be able to find work!'

Howard said, reasonably, 'These are the only Earth clothes I could afford –'

'I'M NOT TALKING ABOUT YOUR EARTH CLOTHES.' The big woman rose and made her heavy way to Howard's chair. She leaned over him, for effect, and poked her sausage-thick finger in his frail, feathery chest. 'I'M TALKING ABOUT YOUR FACE.' She smiled. It struck fear in his heart. 'I've seen a million guys like you.'

'I doubt it –'

'Oh, don't you doubt it, sonny. You think that by lookin' controversial you're never gonna find a job. Just go on collectin' unemployment forever and livin' happy on the public dole!'

'Do I look happy to you?'

'Well you got another think comin', boy. 'Cause Coramae always places her interviewees!' She grinned at him. Howard felt himself shrinking back in his chair. No, he thought. I'm tired of being pushed around. The duck stops here.

'You can't talk to me like that!' he snapped. Howard began to snarl. He reared back and doubled his fists. He confronted her eyeball to eyeball.

She laughed. 'You don't scare me. I'm gonna find you a job that'll wipe that look off your face, little whatever-you-is!'

She stood up and looked thoughtful. 'In fact I got something just right.'

She turned to her desk, moving into Howard's full view her mammoth posterior. It was an inviting target. Howard accepted the invitation. He reared back, jaws wide, and plunged forward –

His bill came down on a sheet of paper. 'Here. Show this to the man at the address on the top. You're gonna take to this job like a duck takes to water!' Coramae, once more triumphant, flicked her hand dismissively. 'Now get!'

Howard got, glad to be out of there. Never mind the abuse, the insults, the taunts, the intimidation – he was starting to get tired of the duck jokes. Who isn't? But that was his fate, and the fate of those who would follow his story.

The sheet fed him – literally – by the fearsome Coramae directed Howard to an establishment named Hot Tub Fever. Howard had never seen anything like it, even on Duck World, where public baths were quite common and beautifully maintained. (That's because, for ducks, water is a necessity, both for proper hygiene and for the general physical and emotional well-being of the citizenry. Americans, of course are different; they need public access to water only for purposes of spending money and fantasizing, i.e., tossing pennies and making wishes.) Hot Tub Fever, needless to say, was not a public bath.

At least, not like the ones on Howard's home planet, which were maintained by the city. This was maintained by its owner, a fat and faintly repulsive man who wore the perpetual leer of a stupid person straining to understand a dirty joke. Howard presented his papers. The owner threw a bathrobe at him to 'suit up'.

'Ova dare,' the owner said, indicating a pile of towels. 'Keep an eye on the Love Suites and make sure they got towels.'

It was gibberish to Howard, until he began making rounds

of the place. The Love Suites were in fact a series of hot tub cubicles. Howard reached the first one and knocked on the flimsy plywood door.

'Mmmmuhh-mphh fuuh,' came from within.

Howard shrugged and opened the door.

Inside were a man and woman, up to their necks in hot water and doing the best to eat each other's mouths. Howard realized, with a shock, that this was some sort of sexual activity. He tossed a towel onto the wooden sitting ledge, muttered, 'Sorry,' and closed the door.

Such was his routine for about an hour. Sometimes the couples were not so much eating each other's mouths as doing . . . well, something else . . . and other times they seemed content to simply splash around or loll against the side. Howard quickly grew morose. Never mind that there was something tacky about the whole setup, that the lovemaking humans were the opposite of erotically attractive, and that the whole joint smelled of disinfectant. What broke Howard's spirit was the fact that tossing towels at hairless apes in tubs was not his idea of a glorious intergalactic adventure.

He was brooding on this, hoping for an excuse to escape, when the owner called after him, 'Hey, shorty!'

'It's Howard, thank you,' the duck replied.

'Howard Thankyou? I don't care if it's Howard Cosell. We got a plugged-up air-jet in number eleven.'

Howard looked at him with an expression of keen uninterest.

'And . . .?'

'Oh. 'And.' Nice.' The owner moved from behind his counter and, with surprising quickness, bent down and seized the hapless bird. 'You want 'and?' I'll give you 'and'. AND, since you're supposed to be the water expert I asked the agency for, you are gonna fix it!'

The man carried the stunned ('WAAAAK??') fowl down a narrow corridor and kicked open the door to number eleven.

'Maintenance!' the owner called, and flung the duck through the air. Howard had just enough time to squawk, 'NO! WAAK! I CAN'T SWIM!' before – (Wait a minute. What was that? A duck who can't swim? Yes – stunning confirmation, as if one was needed, of Phil Blumburtt's evolutionary theory. The ducks of Duck World were land creatures; they (Howard is just about to splash down) had evolved beyond the pond-swimming and river-cruising stage aeons ago. Howard was as inherently unable to swim as the slob who threw him in the tub was to swing through trees.)

– splashing down.

The water was very warm, almost hot. Howard sank to the floor amid a writhing forest of human legs. He hit bottom and saw immediately the air jet in question. A wash cloth had got jammed inside it. He grabbed the cloth and yanked it out. The air shot out at him, blasting a bazooka-worthy charge of bubbles into his face. Desperately, his little lungs ready to pop, he jumped.

He broke the surface choking, gasping, and clutching the wash cloth like recovered treasure. The two people in the tub didn't miss a beat, but kept right on expressing their affection and desire for one another by trying to consume each other's tongues.

'Don't mind me,' the duck said. They didn't.

It took Howard a few minutes to dry off, during which he made up his mind as to what he would do. Then, he did it. He hunted down the owner, whom he found fishing a bra out of a hot mud pit called the 'Lava of Love'. Fate had been kind; the man's back was facing the duck's front.

When Howard was a teenage duckling, he and his friends used to wait for rain, then find a slick, flat expanse, like a tiled pavement or patio. The young ducks would then take a running leap onto the wet surface and slide along using the natural ski-like properties of their broad webbed feet. It was the perfect teen sport; fun, wet, and it drove their mothers crazy.

It all came back to him now. Howard took a loping start, leapt onto the wet tiles that surrounded the mud bath and skidded like a madman right at the owner. The duck cried, 'Maintenance!' and let the creep have it with a good swift kick. The man pitched forward into the mud with a satisfyingly horrible plop.

'I quit!' Howard said. The look on the owner's face – half outrage, half disbelief, all mud – suggested that he would accept Howard's resignation.

Seven

It is exhilarating to quit.

Say you're a duck. Why a duck? Why not. You deserve better treatment, or you don't like the things being done in your name. Your boss is a goon and his business is a sleaze-hole. So you walk. For once, your actions are equal to your beliefs. Having sold the best part of yourself for low cash down and easy, affordable (for your employer) payments, you suddenly repossess it, all contracts cancelled. You are again whole – sort of – and supercharged by anger, impervious to the fat slob's displeasure. You feel drunk on righteousness.

The hangover arrives about two hours later. Say you're still a duck. You are still you, the world has not stood up and applauded, and the needs you had when you went to work are still there after you walk out. Now say you're not a duck – in which case, with luck, those needs can be minimalized, at least for a while.

Now say you're Howard the Duck. Now those needs include just about everything, except a lousy suit of second-hand kids' clothes and a battered overnight bag.

Howard (a duck) stomped around town for a little while, muttering to himself about on-the-job degradation and patting himself on the back for having the guts to waddle out. After a while though, he began to realize that he was right back where he'd started from and not a mile closer to home.

Then, on cue, night fell – not with a bang, but a melancholy twilight whimper. It was a moody Howard that walked the streets in the Cleveland gloaming ([ME (Sc) gloming, fr. OE gloming, fr. gom twilight; akin to OE glowan to glow]: TWILIGHT, DUSK – Webster's Seventh New Collegiate

Dictionary), a solitary ducklike figure silhouetted against the deepening purple sky. The noises of night-time urban America, a veritable Symphony of the City, began to drift through the cooling air.

A distant siren. A flutter of laughter from an open window. The percussive music of bottles being opened, ice cubes being scooped, soda being poured, tee many martoonies being drinkied and winkied. Somewhere, the evocative echo of a dog, barking. Somewhere else, the poignant pop-shatter of two perpetrators with a screwdriver, breaking the window of a BMW and lifting someone's Blaupunkt. Howard could hear it all – a woman sighing; a car's brakes squealing; a kid walking past with a radio the size of a washing machine, playing ('Gonna do a thang/Gonna DO A THANG/GONNA DO A THANG/GONNA do a thang . . .').

Howard meandered glumly through a commercial section of downtown Cleveland, not sure to which place he was going or what thang he was gonna do. Passing pedestrians swerved around him even as they stared. The street lights of the city flickered on in dull gold and chilly blue-green, casting distorted duck-shadows as he walked. A bus, roaring by, showed a line of fluorescent-lit faces gaping down at him. He envied them. They belonged. They had homes and a destination, jobs and a hot meal waiting. They had clothes that fitted. They could go out for pizza with members of their own species.

'Arnold, sounds like good news for Ohio hunters and, well, kinda bad news for local ducks . . .'

Howard thought he was hallucinating. But he had stopped beside a discount appliance place, its window alive with a dozen identical colour images of a news broadcast. On the big and little screens, in various shades of orange and flesh, a chiselled-faced anchor had sent it to a local reporter in the field. The TV journalist in jacket and tie was interviewing a plaid-clad hunter brandishing a shotgun. To Howard the weapon might as well have been field artillery.

'That's right, Bob,' the reporter said. 'This season the Wildlife Commission has actually doubled the limit on ducks.' He held the mike up to the hunter. 'With me is Mr Earl McDowell of the Ohio State Duck Killing Commission. Earl – ducks. Shooting them. More now?'

'Yes indeed, Arnold,' said the droopy-faced hunter, completely without expression. 'The situation, or what have you, is one where you can shoot twice as many ducks as before in a legal way.'

Howard felt the bottom fall out of his stomach.

'And what are Earl McDowell's feelings about that?' the reporter asked with a grin.

'I'm absolutely delighted,' the hunter said, grim as an undertaker. 'The truth is that the state of Ohio is endangered by there being an over-running of its waterways by the duck element. So this increase in the limit has a beneficial effect on the entire ecological balance of the . . . uh . . . situation.'

'Which means you're looking forward to blasting twice as many of our local ducks out of the sky as before . . .'

'That's correct.'

'Earl – pain. Does it hurt the animal when he's shot?'

'Oh, hell, yes. I mean I suppose so.'

The reporter turned to the camera, gave a little smile, and said, 'As the song goes, "Be kind to your fine feathered friends . . . For a duck might be somebody's mother."' He laughed. 'Unfortunately, somebody's mother could well find herself looking down the business end of a double-barrelled –'

Howard heard a gunshot.

He started, flapped, squawked ('SQUAWKK!') and whirled. He flattened himself against the window, cop-show style, and looked frantically about for cover. He was unarmed and defenceless, they'd doubled the limit, and it would hurt . . .

His eye caught the form of a hot rod barrelling down the street, and a second noise confirmed that it had been only the car backfiring – just one more rim shot from the percussion section in the Symphony of the City.

'I'm not takin' any chances,' Howard muttered. With a fearful look in both directions, he grabbed his bag and ran. When he came to an alley, he ducked in.

On the run from everyone and no one. Surrounded by an alien species on a planet he'd never even heard of. 'This is it,' Howard thought, pausing for breath against a cold wall. 'This is the perfect metaphor for the duck condition.' Estranged from himself and mad at everyone else, imprisoned for no crime, in a place he had nothing to do with.

Howard the Duck; trapped in a world he never made.

However. One thing Howard knew on this planet was alleys. They were all the same – at least in this city. This one looked exactly like the one he'd landed in (however long ago that had been), complete with a garage-like factory building blaring some sort of electronic-sounding noise. He stepped slowly down the chilly, dark street. A single bare bulb over the rear basement entrance to a store gave dismal, inadequate lighting. There were garbage cans, refuse, a big discarded easy chair . . .

In fact, this was it – the precise alley he had landed in the day before. The chair he fell on, the car seat he bounded off when he repelled Beverly's attackers, the wooden club Billy tried to clobber him with – all of Howard's Earth history was contained in this dreary stretch of backstreet.

Well, almost all. Beverly wasn't here.

He missed her.

The thought of her awoke in his smallish duck breast a faint but palpable tug of longing. She had been nice to him. Unlike most of the other homo sapiens to whom he had been introduced, she had made no conscious effort to beat his brains out. And she wasn't bad looking, for a hairless ape, although, of course, he being of a different species, of course, than she, of course, it followed that any notion, of course, of –

All right. Admittedly there is, while Howard is sighing and

72

mooning and otherwise clearing away the emotional under-growth in preparation for his first big character-development moment, a certain loose end which could use tying up.

The attentive reader will find him or herself thinking, 'Hold it. Howard "misses" Beverly. He feels a something-something "tug of longing". She "wasn't bad looking", etc. Isn't this getting just a little coy? Are we to understand that he misses her in "that way?" '

Howard missed Beverly. Maybe in some stern, tough-bird sector of his mind he thought he wasn't 'good enough' for her (whatever that meant, under the circumstances), but the alley had evoked a memory, and the memory carried with it certain nice feelings.

In fact, she was not only the first human towards whom he had felt some tenderness since his arrival, she was the first creature he had felt warmly towards in a couple of years. Even back on Duck World, his social life – 'social life,' hell; his dating and love and sex life – had been one gruelling shopping spree through a post-holiday clearance: lots available, all on sale, but nothing decent that fitted.

This one fancied herself a writer, and smugly threw mis-used words in his face like confetti; that one identified herself as a businessduck, and handed out fatuous inspirational-sales-conference clichés more often than her card; the other one was a poet and throbbed with pity for every-thing from homeless orphans to paper clips. ('Don't you feel sorry for broccoli, in a way?' she asked him on their last date. He said yes.) Then there was the lawyer (beautiful, cheerily amoral, frightening), doctor (pathologically com-petitive, very frightening), commercial producer ('I love dating creatives . . .' – extremely frightening), actress ('Creative types love going out with me . . .' – completely frightening), and ballet dancer (' ').

Naturally, he had blamed himself. These were all perfectly attractive ducks. He was the one at fault. With his bad atti-tude, his cynical jokes, his gloomy outlook, his smelly cigars.

He didn't like any of them because he couldn't like anyone. He was a child. He had refused to grow up – look how long it had taken him to get a real job – and had come to resent all those around him who had not had that pathetic problem.

Now, idly shuffling around this miserable alley in Cleveland, prodding empty soda cans and kicking an old tyre with his webbed foot, Howard thought of Bev – and caught a glimmer of something nice inside himself. He liked Bev. He was capable of liking someone worth liking. Maybe he had not been wrong about all those awful dates! Maybe he had just gone out with a string of objectively, verifiably, unambiguously dreadful ducks!

The possibility that he was neither victim nor stupid and boring stirred within him a third option. A year's-long pall of sullenness and defeatism lifted a little in the heart and mind of Howard the Duck. 'Maybe I'm not so bad,' he thought with increased duckly vigour. 'Maybe Number One is worth looking out for.' He paced the godawful alley, possessed by a long-forgotten feeling. He – if only just a little, behind his own back – liked himself! And he wanted to be of service to someone.

Oh, not just anyone – he still would rather be left alone than have anything to do with 99% of the duckly race. But there were certain parties – Bev, for example – who were worth some effort and care.

Howard began talking aloud to himself. He had to raise his voice to hear what he was saying over the din from that damn factory. 'I'm gonna be a different duck from now on,' he said – pacing briskly! Hands working behind his back! 'I'm tired of shufflin' along, waitin' for the next disaster. Gotta find Bev, though. Definitely gotta find Bev.'

The first thing to do was light up the stogie. He pulled from his pocket one of his few remaining Quackanudos, struck a match, and puffed it to life. Done. The next thing was to conceive a Bev-finding strategy –

Then it hit him: night-time, the alley – that was no factory.

That was the club. That noise was Beverly's band.

That singing was – her. She. Whatever.

He found the side entrance and swaggered in. His new clothes did the trick – the bouncer barely noticed him as Howard passed by. A duck in duck's clothes was a kid, but a duck in kid's clothes was one of the boys.

'This planet's nuts,' he thought.

Beverly was on stage with Cherry Bomb, wailing at the mike and looking great. She obviously couldn't see the audience through the lights in her eyes, so Howard was able to watch her undetected. He found a place at the bar, but a volley of harsh laughter made him turn and look –

Some overdressed nitwit with a gold earring and his muscle-brained yes-man, were yukking it up with a guy behind the bar who looked like he owned the joint. The latter produced a roll of bills from his pocket.

'Yo, Ginger, here's the bread for the band,' he said, leering. 'Like we agreed, right?'

The man with the earring took it and slipped it into his jacket pocket. 'Yeah, sure. I'll see they get it.'

'Right. Like when?'

All three men laughed. A bystander searching for bad guys would have looked no further. Then the earring said, 'When bodacious Beverly stops holding out. I invited her up to my place tonight for a little career manipulation, know what I'm saying?'

'Yeah, right – she gets the career and you get the manipulation.'

More guffaws. Howard climbed atop a stool and waited. Ginger, impressed with his own guile, nodded as he laughed. It took a moment before he felt the tap on his shoulder. Turning away from the stage, he beheld nothing less than a duck glaring at him, eye to eye.

'I don't like the way you're talking about Beverly,' Howard said. He felt reckless. Fighting back against the hot tub owner had reawakened his innate physical irascibility.

He decided to go for broke. 'And I want the money you owe 'em.'

Ginger Moss, whose name confirmed the impression he gave of a pungent, primitive (and faintly slimy) life-form, gave a short incredulous smirk and turned to his bodyguard/chauffeur. 'What the hell is *that*?'

The bodyguard's name was Ritchie. Big guy. Strong. Ritchie. Real name Richard, but you know. Got his B.A. at the University of Busting Guys in the Face. Graduated *come loud*, okay? He shrugged. 'I told ya about gettin' involved with rock 'n' roll, Ginger. Entertainment types. You're going to be dealing with all kinds of jerks.'

'You're telling me –' Ginger said, then found his arm rudely tapped and his drink tragically spilt all over his nice silk pants. 'Hey –'

'He's not telling you, Ginger,' Howard said, tapping him again. 'I am. I'm not in a real good mood tonight. I want the girls' money. Now. Is this going to be easy, or are we talking trouble?'

Ginger turned to his hired muscle and said, 'Lose this jerk.'

Ritchie was hip to the argot. 'Absolutely.'

So Ritchie like seized Howard and flung him down the bar. The startled duck found himself sliding down the puddle-slicked surface on his stomach, a feathered bowling ball, smashing glasses and overturning little bowls of horrible claylike peanuts. As he slid, Howard could see Beverly glance up, squint, and with a look of mild disgust go on playing – she must have thought this just an ordinary bar room brawl.

Ginger slapped Ritchie on the back and again the three men shared a raucous laugh. The same bystander in the bar that night might have thought: It must be great to be a bad guy – they laugh so much more than protagonists.

Then again, they don't laugh for long at any given time, because the hero often – as happened now – intervenes. Howard pulled himself back up onto his feet, and stalked down the bar with measured tread and steely eyes. If he had had a sixgun strapped to his hip he'd have looked remarkably like the great duck film star, Gary Coop, in the classic western, *Bad Day At Quack Rock*. Having no pistol, however, he had to resort to other methods.

First to neutralize Ritchie. Howard swiped a wet towel off the bartender's shoulder and slapped the big galoot across the face. Then, summoning up every half-baked scrap of his esoteric so-called knowledge, he gave forth the Quack Fu Cry of Ultimate Self-Abandonment ('HEEEYAAAA-HA!') and kicked the guy in the head.

'Hey –!' the club's owner protested.

Howard grabbed a bottle and brought it down over the owner's head. That individual lost what we may laughingly refer to as his consciousness and sank, slowly, onto the floor.

Ginger, meanwhile, seized Howard by his jacket and pinioned him to the bar. Women screamed, men shouted and applauded, everyone backed off, as Ginger reached across the bar and grabbed something.

Howard caught a glimpse. It was an ice pick.

Ginger reared back and brought the pick down in a vicious stab. It hit Howard! Or, rather, it hit where Howard had been – he was able to roll aside at the last millisecond, leaving Ginger an unobstructed stab at the bar itself. The pick stuck in there as Ginger recoiled, shaking his hand from the rude impact. Howard saw his chance.

He grabbed the pick and pried it out. Ginger leapt towards him and Howard repelled him with a semi-perfect Kick of Exemplary Uncoiling, sending the man reeling. Ginger turned, staggered and fell backwards – onto the bar, face up. Howard leaped high! With both hands around the pick! Raising it up as though about to stake a vampire! Which, in a sense, he was! He brought it down with a vicious slash as grown men fainted and some broad screamed –!

There was the solid, nutty sound an ice pick makes when it is deeply embedded in a wooden bar. Hard on that noise came a sort of restrained little shriek from Ginger Moss. His face froze in a rictus of terror – and, slowly, relaxed a bit. He turned his head about an inch to the left, and nearly shattered his eyeballs in an effort to slide them over as far as they could go to see what had happened.

Howard had – deliberately, let's assume – driven his pick through the loop of Ginger's golden earring, affixing it and its wearer, to the top of the bar.

'Only one earring?' Howard said. He was standing on the bar over Ginger's helpless face. He found another ice pick – astounding, in this day of ice cube machines – and gestured with it. 'Maybe if I pierced your other ear –'

'No, no, please!' Ginger yelled.

'Then what about that money?'

'In my pocket! Take it!'

Howard started to reach for the cash, then stopped, and looked at the ice pick in his hand. 'Hmmm . . .'

'What? What? What? What?' Ginger squealed. 'What "hmmmm?"'

'I think the girls want out of their contract with you, Ginger.'

'You got it! They're out! Forget the contract! Listen, everybody! You're witnesses! I'm letting the girls out of the contract!'

'Outstanding,' Howard said, fishing around in the man's jacket until he withdrew the roll of bills. He saw movement off to the side – Ritchie and the bar owner starting to close in. 'Tell them to stay back! If they make one more move, I bite your face. And you're a dead man.'

'Bull!' Ginger said. Then he went pale and queried, 'How come?'

Howard looked up at Ritchie, eyes narrowed, and said, 'Space rabies.'

'GAAH! Space rabies!' Ginger gulped. 'Whazzat?'

'One bite,' Howard said, 'And you buy yourself fifteen minutes of indescribable agony. Then . . . death.'

'Death! Death!'

'Jeez, Ginger,' Ritchie said. 'That could prove fatal.'

Howard left it at that. The crowd parted nervously as the duck walked towards the rear of the club. Howard found the dressing room door and knocked. One of the women in the band answered.

'Beverly here?' Howard asked.

After the requisite staring and uh-ing and you're-really-a-duck-ing, Caldonia let Howard in and introduced him to Ronette and K.C. Beverly emerged from a room in the rear, suprised.

'Hi, ducky,' she said tenderly.

Howard's gruffness was forced. He was moved. 'Hi, doll.'

They gazed at each other for a moment, duck and doll, until another figure burst out from the back room.

'Howard. Oh, thank God you're back.' It was Phil Blumburtt, more manic than ever. 'I've been looking into how you got here and I may have something –'

Ronette intercepted him and shoved him back into the rear room. 'Give, 'em some time together first, Blumburtt, okay?'

'Huh? Yeah, sure, I can be sensitive –'

Howard and Bev had continued to look at each other. Now she sat on an amplifier and he went over to her. She smoothed his ruffled head feathers.

'How's the world been treating you?' she asked.

'Guess.'

'I was worried about you.' She said, with difficulty, 'I missed you, Howard.'

He shrugged. 'Sex appeal, I guess. Some guys got it, some don't.' Then he grew serious. 'Bev, listen . . . I'm sorry I walked out on you. You're the only friend I got here.'

'Do you need a place to stay tonight?'

'Well, now that you ask . . .'

Blumburtt burst back in. 'All done? Good. Howard, listen. I've been working on the mystery of your arrival. I've talked to some astrolo-physicists – the ones who believe that the Aztecs came from Mars.'

Howard looked at Phil, then at Beverly. 'What's he doing here?'

'He and Ronette have sort of gotten back together,' she said. Ronette, from across the room, said, 'Bev, I don't know who's more desperate for dates, you or me.'

'You,' Howard said.

'Ha, ha, good one, Howard,' Blumburtt said. 'Anyway. These guys concluded that you didn't land here on earth – you were here already!'

'What?'

'You arrived in a space craft millions and millions of years ago. You remained a mummy frozen in ice, until the pollution of a river thawed you out. Then –'

'Go away! Just leave me alone!'

'I know. I know. It's improbable. I don't buy it either. So I did some more research, and I found that the primitive Samoans worshipped an ancient race of large DUCKS!' Blumburtt dodged to one side as Howard threw an ashtray at him. 'Right. You mean, so what? Exactly. But today I got a real lead! And tonight I'm supposed to be getting concrete evidence as to how you got here! Woops, what time is it?' He looked at his watch. It had three sets of hands, two digital readouts, a stop watch and a calculator and told the time in twelve time zones and on four other planets. 'Excuse me one second, gotta make a call.' He scurried outside to the pay phone.

Howard and the women, meanwhile, left the club. On the street K.C. said, 'Hey, do we get money tonight, or what? Where's that slime Ginger?'

'I think he was part of that fight out there,' Caldonia said.

'Oh, right, I forgot,' Howard said, and produced the roll of money. 'I persuaded Ginger to give you this.' He handed it to Beverly.

The girls gaped. Beverly said, 'Ducky . . . I can't believe it!'

'Oh,' Howard added, brutally nonchalant. 'And I got him to agree to step aside as your manager.'

'What?' Ronette yelped. 'You got rid of Ginger? How?'

Howard shrugged. 'Diplomacy, persuasion, and Quack Fu.'

'Mr Duck,' Ronette said. 'I don't know where you're from, but you're wonderful.'

She kissed the top of his head. What's wrong with that? The others tried to also, but Howard waved them off. Just then Phil burst out the door and joined them.

'Howard. Good news. I'm going to meet with my colleague. Secretly. This is big – very big. He's going to bring . . . the feather.'

'Huh?'

'If the feather he has matches yours,' Blumburtt said, approaching Howard slowly, 'it'll be the answer to . . . all . . . your–'

'Matches mine . . .?' Howard recoiled. 'NO! KWAAAK! STAY BACK!'

Too late. Phil leapt in and plucked a single white feather from Howard's tail. The duck spun and advanced, mad as hell and not willing to take it any more. The women held him back, offering soothing words to Howard and dark glares to the scientist.

Blumburtt was unfazed. 'I'm about to unravel the mystery of your arrival, Howard. Never mind the Nobel Prize that'll be in it for me. I'm strictly interested in science. Why? Because that's the kind of guy I am.'

'You–'

'I know. You're grateful. Hey, no problem. You can thank me later.'

Blumburtt dashed off. The soda bottle Howard threw at him shattered harmlessly against the wall.

Eight

Cleveland in the wee small hours of the morning. Most folks are asleep. Some, victims of insomnia, sigh and stare at the ceiling, or toss, turn and try not to think of that moronic Top Forty song (or, worse, commercial jingle) they happened to hear earlier in the day and which now replays obsessively in the juke box of their mind. How to make it stop? They actually consider counting sheep. Would it be effective? Or too corny for words? They lie there, more wakeful and alert than when they operate the heaviest of machinery, and rack their overactive brains for an alternative.

An excellent sheep-alternative is ducks. To begin counting them, one could do worse than pay a visit to Beverly Switzler's loft. She had one. It – he – Howard 'the' Duck – stayed with her after the confrontation in the bar. 'Make yourself at home, ducky,' she said and he did.

They had stopped at an all-night, all-everything drugstore for a fast raid on the racks of cheap clothes and Howard had come away with a pair of children's pyjamas – flannel, soft and cuddly, in a pattern of small, anatomically incorrect ducks. It was cute – perhaps too cute. Anatomically correct Howard now sat at Beverly's piano, tapping out hard-edged little tunes.

'I hate these pyjamas, you know,' he said.

'It was all they had in your size.' Beverly emerged from the bathroom in a Foxy Lady T-shirt. The fox was loose in the duck coop. She paused and admired the duck's ticklage of the eighty-eight. 'Where'd you learn to play like that?'

'High school.' He unrolled a little blues riff with the right hand – a little Fats Waddler, a little Dave Brubeak. 'We had a group called Howard and the Heartbreakers.' He told her about his ducklinghood influences – Chick Corea, Herbie Hancock, and so forth – and about how he discovered rock 'n' roll. 'I even wrote some songs,' he said. He pounded out a few chords and sang, 'Hey hey hey/I was born to waddle/Down in Duxie/On a Sunday morning/With one foot in the grave/And one hand on the throttle/I was born to waddle . . .'

'Not bad, Howard,' she laughed. 'Maybe you should be our manager.'

'Very funny. But that's not funny.'

'Why not?' She thought about it for a second. 'You might be just the thing we need. Kind of an off-the-wall influence.'

'Off the wall?' He banged the keys with both fists. It sounded a little like DeCoy Tyner. 'I'm off more than the wall! I'm off the world! My world! My whole life is totally off! I've got problems of my own, sweetheart, so don't go making any plans for me –'

Beverly shrugged that off as she walked to the bed. 'I think you'd make a great manager. All the girls like you, too. I'm gonna suggest it tomorrow.'

'Forget it!' Howard spun on the bench and faced her, his cigar waggling up and down in his mouth as he spoke. He was running out of Quackanudos – one more headache. 'I'm through looking for jobs here. It's no use my trying to assimilate. I've got to get back to my own kind. So the next question is, how?'

Bev bent over to turn down the bed. Howard, whose eyes were already in the neighbourhood of her body, saw her from the rear. And let's face it, duck or no duck, some things are inherently pleasing. He whistled.

'You are the worst,' she said. 'Come on, ducky, we'll watch some tube.' She climbed in and patted the other side – his side – of the bed.

Howard felt that age-old buzz. He gave a couple of Groucho lifts of his eyebrows, or whatever those things were above his eyes and gave his head feathers a quick fluff. As he strolled over to where she sat up, smiling, she said, 'You know, Howard, my life's really changed since you fell into it.'

'Yeah, well, I'm glad somebody's happy . . .'

'And if I can get my career back on course, I'll only have one thing to worry about.'

He climbed between the sheets. 'What's that?'

'Men.' She shrugged. It was a gesture that spoke volumes. 'I can't seem to find the right one.'

Howard threw her his never-fails droop-lidded sex-killer look. It was a gesture that spoke one, at most two sentences. 'Maybe it's not a man you should be looking for.'

She pursed her lips and looked mischievous. 'You think I might find happiness in the animal kingdom, ducky?'

'I was thinking of the duck kingdom, actually.' He waved an airy hand, Mr Completely Calm and In His Element. The ducks he'd gone out with always bought it. Yeah, but look at the kind of ducks he'd gone out with . . . 'Like they say, doll, love is strange. We could give it a try . . .'

'Okay.' She reached out a finger and ran it along his arm. 'Let's go for it, Big Bird.'

Howard, staring at her slowly stroking finger, gulped, 'What do you mean, "okay"? Go for . . . what?' She snuggled in close. He hadn't expected this. And he didn't know what to expect. 'Uh, look, Bev . . . I'm pretty tired –'

'But you're just so incredibly soft and cuddly . . .' She walked her fingers up his stomach. He watched her hand advance as though it were a third party in bed with them. Working for her.

'Uh, Bev, look,' he stammered. 'Let's be realistic. This could never work. Say we go to your place a couple times. What happens when we decide to go to mine? It's in another galaxy! Think of the cab fare! Plus you're three feet taller than me –'

Bev unbuttoned the top button of Howard's duck-swarming pyjamas. 'I don't mind,' she murmured. 'I just can't resist your intense animal magnetism.'

84

She caressed his chest – and the thing Howard had hoped wouldn't happen, did. His head feathers suddenly popped up. If she had been a duck, he'd have been mortally embarrassed, except, of course, he wouldn't have been embarrassed at all and would have been too busy doing other things. But she was not remotely a duck.

'But . . . where'll it all end?' he said, trying to appeal to her reason. 'Marriage? Kids? A house in the suburbs?'

She unbuttoned several more buttons. It was all he could do to follow after her playful fingers and button them up again. 'Let's face it,' she said. 'It's fate.'

'No, it's not,' he said, as though that made sense. He tried another tack. 'I should have told you before. There's somebody back home . . . her name's Wendie . . . we're sort of engaged . . .'

(Howard had to force himself to tell this little white lie. The truth was he'd gone out with Wendie a few times, but the idea of their being engaged was too hilarious to believe and too awful to contemplate. She simply wasn't his type. They saw '*Beverly Hills Cod*.' She'd loved it, he'd hated it. Howard read Norman Mallard and listened to *Squawking Heads*. Wendie's idea of reading was the front page of *The Wall Street Gerbil*. And as for music – show tunes! She knew all the words to every song of *La Cage Au Fowl*! Still, Bev didn't have to know any of that. 'It would kill her if –'

'She'll never know . . .' Beverly moved closer until she was almost on top of him. Howard pulled the blankets up to his neck.

'I can't – I've got a headache!'

'Think of me as aspirin,' she sighed, and moved in for the kiss. Howard felt stymied, trapped, turned on, freaked out. What should he do? She was three inches away and closing fast –

She stopped.

She started laughing like hell.

'Oh, Howard, I really got you! You thought I was serious!'

Relief. It turned his legs to jelly. 'Me?' he quacked weakly. 'I knew you were kidding all along . . .'

'You were scared to death.'

'Not "scared," exactly,' he said unconvincingly. 'A little worried, maybe. I mean, the moral ramifications and all. Right?'

'Right.' She leaned over and turned off the bedside lamp. Then she turned to him. 'Whatever that means. Anyway, good night, sweet ducky.' She kissed him lightly. It was very sweet and very, very nice –

– but then the lights went on. The place went nuts. Phil Blumburtt appeared from behind a screen that separated the sleeping area from the rest of the loft, accompanied by some stranger. The stranger was aghast.

'My God!' the stranger gasped. 'This defies all the laws of nature!'

'No it doesn't!' Howard cried.

'This is unspeakable!'

'No it isn't! You can speak it!'

'But . . . these two creatures are –'

'– friends!' Howard yelled. 'Just good friends!'

Beverly's eyes flashed as she confronted the nutbar palaeontologist. 'Phil –'

'Ah, sorry,' Blumburtt mumbled. 'Listen, the door was open and we heard talking, so –'

'Who the hell is he?' Howard demanded, indicating the gaping stranger.

'This is Carter.' Blumburtt made the introductions. Carter still looked appalled but managed to shake hands and control himself. 'Carter works in Spectroscopic Emission Control,' Blumburtt explained.

'I don't need another lunatic pulling my feathers out,' Howard said. 'Beat it.'

'No, Howard, please, I'm serious this time.' Blumburtt gestured to Carter. 'Show him.'

Carter produced from his jacket a small plastic case. With

an air of mystery he opened it and removed a single feather. Blumburtt held up the one he'd plucked from Howard earlier. They looked alike.

'I tested them,' Phil explained. 'They're both from you, Howard.'

'Great!' Howard leaped off the bed, one angry duck wearing a hundred cute little duckies. 'Now it's my turn. Lemme see if I can pull two different hairs off you and we'll see if they match—'

'Howard, please, you have to listen to me. I know how you got here.'

Even Howard was stunned. 'Yeah?'

Carter had brought a VCR and a video cassette. Everyone set up in the living room area – Beverly huddled in a blanket, Phil Blumburtt fidgeting in a chair. Howard, out of the damn pyjamas and into his other clothes, leaned against the couch and looked sceptical but interested.

Carter slipped the tape into the machine and said, 'When Phil first told me about you, I thought he'd flipped out on drugs.'

'He thought I was wacko!' Blumburtt laughed, looking at Bev and Howard. 'Can you believe that!' They didn't laugh. Apparently they could believe it.

'But the dates were too coincidental,' Carter continued. 'I thought, What if this alien fowl, or duck-like bird, or whatever it is—'

'Watch it,' Howard snarled.

'– What if this creature arrived on earth because of our experiments?' He looked at them. 'I work at Aerodyne. It's an astrophysics laboratory. We do research, defence work – super-secret, billion-dollar, phoney-baloney stuff. That's off the record, by the way. That last baloney part. Anyway, on the night of September 8 –'

'Isn't that the night Howard landed?' Beverly asked.

'Right. And that night we were working late at the lab with Walter Jenning. He's our research supervisor. We were using the laser spectroscope.' Carter pushed a button and the tape began. 'This was shot during the experiment. Don't ask me why.'

The picture on the TV screen was of a modern scientific lab, a big open room crowded with measuring devices and computers, all arrayed around a gigantic instrument resembling a conventional telescope. A section of the ceiling had been retracted to reveal the starry night sky. Tracings slid and jumped and jogged on various oscilloscope screens, numbers scrolled from bottom to top on green and amber computer monitors, dials turned, red lights glowed, meters metered, gauges gauged. The mammoth device in the centre resembled a huge ray gun directed towards the heavens. A dozen men in white lab coats checked readings and adjusted dials. All the men wore goggles and made excellent salaries at taxpayer's expense.

At the control panel of the main device stood a grave, intense man in his late thirties. 'That's Dr Jenning,' Carter said. 'This procedure was supposed to be a routine measurement. We were just trying to get baseline readings of the density of the gases that cover the star Alpha Centauri. But something happened.'

On the screen, some of the scientists seemed to start. Everyone turned towards the spectroscope on which an amber warning light had begun to blink. 'Dr Jenning lost control of the Laser Spectroscope. It began to re-orientate itself. And we couldn't stop it.'

They could see it on the tape: the giant scope began to pivot slowly, its base turning and its shaft shifting downward. The scientists hovering around it looked worried.

'At first we thought it was a computer malfunction. But we weren't getting any readings. Then we realized that it was being controlled remotely – some unknown force was redirecting the laser beam from its original target.' Carter looked at Howard and said, 'It hit your planet instead.'

'My planet?' Howard griped. 'It hit my living room!'

On the screen, the spectroscope began to vibrate. Other equipment in the lab began to shudder, too, and the assembled staff looked frantically around, helpless. Carter said, 'When the beam hit you, Howard, you must have been caught up in a massive energy inversion. Then – there. See?' The scope began to glow, and was suddenly obliterated in a blinding white flash. 'The inversion literally dragged you through space back down here to the source of the power.' The glow subsided, and the scientists could be seen lowering their goggles, gaping at the machinery and at each other in silent amazement.

Suddenly Carter said, 'Right there. Top of the screen. That's all we saw.' It was a single white duck feather, drifting lazily down through the open ceiling. 'We didn't know at the time that the rest of Howard landed in an alley two miles away.' He shut off the tape. The room was silent.

Then Howard walked over and grabbed his coat.

'Where you going, ducky?' Beverly yawned.

'To that lab,' the duck groused. 'For a little quackfest with good old Dr Jenning.'

'Now? It's four o'clock in the morning.'

'Well, he's there,' Carter said. 'They've all been working round the clock since this happened. But I'll have to call ahead.' He went to the phone and punched out a number.

'Good,' Howard said. 'And after our talk, I'll just hop on this thing. All we have to do is throw it into reverse, right?'

'Throw it where?' Carter said, the phone to his ear.

'Into reverse! Shift gears! Hit the rewind button! Turn it around so it sends me back home!'

Carter looked at Blumburtt. 'Well, we hadn't really considered reversing the process . . .'

'It could work!' Blumburtt said excitedly. 'If you could generate a strong enough Gauss wave, you could rectify the Helmholtz charge and amplify the quark potential enough to reverse the ion spin and triple the inertia!'

Carter said, 'What are you talking about?'

'I have no idea,' Blumburtt said. 'I made it up. Come on, I'm a palaeontologist. But couldn't it work? Couldn't you send Howard back?'

His friend flexed his lips, thoughtful. 'Possibly. The reflex mode might provoke a total reversal . . . oh, sorry. Dr Jenning? Carter. I've just met something – someone, actually – I think you'll be very interested in . . .'

Explanations were tendered, 'What's?' were exclaimed, 'Yes, sir, a duck's' were insisted. Finally, arrangements were made and Beverly dressed. A few minutes later the four were in Blumburtt's van, en route to the lab.

Nine

In the front of the van, Carter and Phil Blumburtt fantasized about the use of the laser spectroscope for interstellar travel. Not only would they be able to send Howard back home, but a continual link between the two planets might be established. The possibilities were staggering.

Carter speculated on the gains that might be made in the specific areas of medicine and linguistics, as well as engineering and evolutionary science. Blumburtt's vision was no less bold. He foresaw a vigorous scientific and cultural exchange between the humans of Earth and the ducks of Duck World, to be described clearly and wittily by him in a twelve-part PBS series for which he would also write the 'companion volume' (illustrated in colour), the perfect holiday gift. And the perfect subscription bonus for viewers who pledge one hundred dollars. He would gladly consent to be taped for a Pledge Week pitch and happily autograph the first ten, twenty, fifty, three hundred copies.

Meanwhile, in the rear of the truck, amidst tools, spare tyres, and assorted Museum of Natural History junk, Bev watched with mounting melancholy as Howard checked the contents of his overnight bag.

'You sure you packed my Hot Tub Fever bathrobe?' he asked. She nodded, unable to speak. 'Oh, and thanks for these –' He flipped through a small sheaf of photographs of her and Cherry Bomb. 'The guys back home'll never believe this.'

'I just hope they let you take a carry-on bag . . .' she managed.

Howard looked at her in the dimness. Her voice betrayed

her feeling. How could he explain what he felt? 'Bev . . . I really don't belong here –'

'I know.'

'– and if they can send me, I gotta go.'

She forced a smile and looked away. 'I was just remembering when I first met you. I said some pretty dumb things about pets.'

'Forget it.'

'And now I'm remembering all the other stuff I said.' She paused. 'And didn't say.'

'Yeah, well –'

'I mean, you certainly didn't turn out to be a pet.' She wiped away a tear. 'And you're a lot more than just a friend . . .'

'Aw, look, Bev,' Howard said, fidgeting. 'I'm not a real sentimental guy . . .' He took her hand in his. Hers had five fingers; his had four. So there you were. 'But I have to admit – when I look at you I have second thoughts about leaving . . .'

The van slowed and began to turn left into a driveway.

'We're here,' Carter said.

COVERAGE-IN-DEPTH INSERT 3
Aerodyne: A Corporate History

Aerodyne, Inc., of Shaker Heights, Ohio, is a privately owned research laboratory specializing in high-energy beam transmission, wide-range force-field generation, long-range digital telemetric processing, and 'human-plant conversationalistics.'

Located on a sprawling, beautifully landscaped four-acre campus near one of America's most dynamic urban centres, Aerodyne came into being in 1981, the brainchild of Douglas ('Doug') Aerodopoulos, a former Army weapons procurement officer, and Dyna Koznowskievicz, a 'plant hypnotist' moonlighting on a Pentagon night-time cleaning crew. The story of their unlikely partnership and the success of their venture stands as yet another monument to the new entrepreneurial spirit of spirited enterprise and innovational zeal that has flourished zealously all over the place during 'The Age of It's Okay To Be Ambitious Again.'

Nearing mandatory retirement in 1980, Aerodopoulos faced the crisis of his career. Not one defence industry contractor, or sub-contractor, or supplier had had the simple courtesy to offer him the 'consultancy position' traditionally given ex-procurement people when they step down from government employment. After decades of faithful service to the defence industry – authorizing payment of top dollars for A regardless of its actual cost; campaigning enthusiastically for B irrespective of its actual utility – Doug Aerodopoulos was suddenly, in his words, 'John Nobody, who you don't even have to return his damn phone calls.'

The well-oiled revolving door between the private and public sectors, through which so many of Doug's colleagues had passed so smoothly, was suddenly jammed. A man might suffocate in there, waiting for some repair guy from Lockheed or General Dynamics to come along and fix it.

It was during his final week on the job that Aerodopoulos, casually pawing through every document he could lay his hands on at the last minute, discovered that a sum of money larger than usual had somehow slipped through the Pentagon accountants' nets. It had been simply overlooked, and was now lying around gathering dust. Earmarked for Project 'Hi-Ho Silver' (object: the practical use of lasers to dislodge the bridgework and dental fillings of East German guards along the Berlin Wall), a total of sixteen million was missing and presumed spent.

After a series of 'agonizing' informal consultations with his colleagues in both industry and the Pentagon, Aerodopoulos decided he could not supress his innate entrepreneurial zeal – and that it would be unpatriotic for him to even try. He retired four days ahead of schedule, ate the penalty imposed on his pension disbursement for premature retirement, and took the sixteen mil. His goal: to found a firm in which the skills, expertise, and contacts he had gained during thirty-eight years in the weapons business might be enlisted to make America strong, fight Communism, and things like that.

Enter thirty-six-year-old Dyna Koznowskievicz. A self-styled 'botanic therapist,' it was her special talent to coax houseplants and garden vegetables into fuller bloom and more abundant production by reading Kipling to them while playing castanets. Winter was her slow season. In 1980 she was earning extra income as a cleaning lady working the floor of Aerodopoulos's Pentagon office. (A former mental patient diagnosed as being subject to occasional spells of mild schizophrenia, she had no known Communist sympathies and obtained instant security clearance.)

While straightening up around Aerodopoulos's desk one evening, Dyna – 'Dyne' to her friends on the night crews and in the plant kingdom – stumbled across certain documents. Perhaps Doug had left them there accidentally-on-purpose. Perhaps it represented an unconscious effort to undermine what he may have felt, in some deep vestigial ethics-centre of his pineal gland, was a morally-suspect scheme. On the other hand, perhaps he had just got sloppy after knocking back half a bottle of Chivas all day with his secretary in anticipatory celebration. Whichever the case, Dyna took them home to read to her begonias.

Dyna Koznowskiewicz may have been schizophrenic, but she wasn't crazy. The import of these documents was not lost on her plants, let alone her. She approached Aerodopoulos the next day, and with a new entrepreneurial spirit, offered not to send xeroxes to the G.A.O. in exchange for a full partnership in his new spirited entrepreneurial venture.

At first Aerodopoulos offered to buy her out for money or stock. But, as she pointed out, there was no guarantee she would not return in a year, or a few months, or a half-hour, and demand more, and so on, ad infinitum. No, she insisted, she wanted to be part of the business – with an office, secretary, credit card, Mr Coffee and 'nice big ficus trees'. All that, plus the money.

Doug Aerodopoulos was stuck. It was one thing to emerge six months after retirement as head of a brand-new, sixteen-million-dollar company, hungry for feeding at the Defence Department trough. It was another to share its directorship with a cleaning lady. The former he could explain away in the usual manner. He could, for example, refuse to identify the source of his seed money by invoking national security, citing Top Secret classifications, and so forth. But how would he explain this loony's presence in the building, let alone her name under his on the letterhead?

He agreed to meet with Dyna at her apartment for one final negotiation. He arrived after a sleepless night, exhausted and on edge. The place was a jungle of houseplants – spiders, begonias, dracaenas, snakes, peperomiae, everything. You needed a machete to get to the bathroom. Doug shouldered his way to a sofa and fell into it like a corpse pushed into a grave. With a pessimistic sigh he went into his rehearsed speech.

He would put her on the payroll for life, if only she would play the role of a silent partner. She could afford to live anywhere, do anything. The company's classified files would be forever safe from prying investigators. It was a dream setup. She –

She wasn't listening. She was talking baby-talk to the plants.

'Excuse me, Ms Kozna-whoosis,' he said tartly. 'But are we discussing business here or what?'

'This is my business,' she said. 'This is my true job.' As the spirited entrepreneur listened with open mouth, she explained her special talent and accomplishments.

A madwoman who read poetry to houseplants in close association with a Pentagon research lab? Aerodopoulos laughed. He felt ten years younger. He rose, embraced the woman, and said, 'I think we've got a deal, partner.'

His delighted colleague fancied the name 'Koznowskiedoug' for their business, but he was able to dissuade her. Thus 'Aerodyne' was born. Its first year was touch and go. The military-industrial complex is like Harvard: it's tough to get in, but almost impossible to fail once you make it. Aerodyne benefited from its principal founder's ample connections and canny reading of the defence appropriations landscape.

But perhaps the biggest break for the spirited, entrepreneurial young company came in the form of a six-million-dollar research contract. It was with the U.S. Army, and called for 'the investigation of the possibility of man-plant communication and the feasibility of the use thereof for purposes of national defence'.

That project was still underway when the Howard the Duck/Jenning episode occurred. Fortunately, all the personnel involved in it were spared any injury. Dyna Koznowskievicz – who comprised the entire research staff – had stayed home that week to watch the soaps.

As they pulled up to the guardhouse, Carter frowned. He turned to Howard and Beverly and shrugged. 'The barrier is up. That's weird. Better get down anyway, just in case . . .'

'After you,' Howard said, holding up an edge of a tarpaulin. Bev crawled under it. As the truck pulled to a stop, he ducked – all right, he crawled – below the tarpaulin with Bev and waited. Maybe he kibitzed a little with her under there, who knows. It's a free country.

Eyes shifting like a sneaky person's, Phil Blumburtt told Carter to get his pass ready. But no guard emerged. They could have been two guys smuggling a rock singer and duck and driven right in.

'You guys can come out,' Phil called to his passengers. 'For some reason there's no one on duty . . .'

They drove on, around the driveway to the front of the main building. Carter and Blumburtt got out and opened the side door for Howard and Bev. The front door was also unattended. 'This is all wrong,' Carter muttered. They went into the lobby.

It was empty. A warning buzzer was sounding on and off, echoing throughout the corridors beyond. Howard could smell smoke. Carter frowned as he led them briskly through another door under a flashing red light into the hallways of Aerodyne.

The smoke was everywhere, dull white, acrid and lingering. All three humans coughed and Howard had to blink repeatedly. 'Something's happened,' Carter said. He led them on faster into another hall. The buzzer from the lobby had faded, but now they heard buzzers, bells, a repetitive muted whistle. The offices were deserted. At the end of the hall stood a locked high-security door, with a numerical key pad mounted on the wall. Carter punched in some numbers and the door opened. He had almost forgotten about his guests and moved quickly down the next short hallway towards a door and a sign: SECURITY AREA – PASSES REQUIRED.

They had nearly reached it when it banged open. A figure staggered out of a welter of smoke and noise. Beverly screamed. The man was clutching his face, moaning, 'My eyes! My eyes!' He swayed, stumbled and fell.

The four visitors ran to him. Howard bent over just as the man drew himself up a bit. He pushed his smoke-blackened face into Howard's and gasped, 'My God! It was terrible! We have no right to tamper with the universe!'

'My feelings exactly,' Howard said.

The man fainted. Blumburtt stared in horror, and Beverly looked away, as Howard murmured, 'This don't look good.'

'Come on,' Carter said, and he leaped to the door and yanked it open. He bolted through. The others followed.

They emerged into chaos.

It was the main lab, the one seen on Carter's video tape. There were scientists in their white lab coats, leaning against walls or seated on the floor, gasping in shock or staring blankly; security guards in uniform working fire extinguishers on several small blazes; a secretary near hysteria, babbling on a telephone; men in shirtsleeves and inexpressibly neat ties peering at machines, gently removing panels from computers, adjusting gauges in an effort to assess damage. It was as though a bomb had just gone off in the room.

The smoke seemed to be drifting towards the far wall. As they moved further into the lab Howard followed its flow and beheld a gigantic jagged hole in the rear wall, encompassing the ceiling port where the spectroscope had been aimed at the sky.

A scientist spotted them and ran over, coughing.

'Larry!' Carter called. 'What –'

'Jenning was activating the spectroscope,' the man said. 'We lost control again and . . . I don't know . . . all of a sudden the whole 'scope just blew up! Jenning was right there when it went.' Larry shook his head. 'He caught it full force.'

'Where is he now?'

'Somebody thought they saw him stagger out through this hole. Look at it! Jesus. Anyway, no one knows. He's disappeared.'

Howard took a step past Larry and regarded the giant opening in the wall. 'Something tells me my return flight's going to be delayed . . .'

Larry suddenly gaped and pointed Howard-wards. 'Is that . . . it? Him? Carter – you were right! A creature from ANOTHER WORLD! It's unbelievable. He looks just like a . . . duck!'

'He is a duck,' Carter said. 'Larry, Howard.'

'Charmed,' Howard said.

'He is a duck! Fantastic!'

'So's your old mallard.'

'A duck. Amazing.'

Carter was looking past them towards the gaping hole in the building and out into the night. 'Howard's what we brought down the first time,' he murmured. 'God knows what we've brought down this time . . .'

They heard sirens approaching.

Aerodyne came alive with whirling, blinking red lights, as cop cars and fire trucks pulled up. Firemen leaped down and deployed hoses like huge black snakes throughout the building. Police fanned out, secured the area, and corralled everyone – scientists, security, technicians, secretaries – for questioning. They didn't know what to make of Howard, so they took him to a drafting room for special interrogation. He didn't like it and informed them to that effect repeatedly.

Beverly, meanwhile, answered a number of plodding questions from a young cop who kept giving her the eye. Talking duck in the next room, unexplained explosion and reports of strange energy beams from outer space and this guy comes on. Unbelievable. Finally his commanding officer, a Lieutenant Weber, arrived.

'I want to know why they're harrassing Howard,' Beverly demanded. Weber looked at the cop. 'Who's Howard?'

'He didn't have anything to do with this!' she said. 'He's just an innocent . . . um . . .'

'Bystander,' Weber said, mockingly.

'Duck.'

He looked at the cop. 'Hah?'

'This way, sir,' the cop said.

They went into the drafting room. Weber had no sooner asked the man on the scene, Kirby, about his prisoner, than Howard appeared from behind a desk and started speaking his mind.

'I want to see a lawyer!' he growled. 'I'm protected by the Duck Bill of Rights! I'll sue –!'

'Goddammit, Kirby,' Weber said, eyes on Howard. 'Get the duck suit off this man.'

Beverly said, 'Um –'

'Yes, sir!'

Kirby grabbed Howard with both hands. The cop who had questioned Bev, a youngster named Hanson, stepped up to help. Another officer joined them. And for the next few minutes the air was filled with curses and cuss words, both duck and human.

They could be transcribed here, but to what end? Such words – in print, if not in person – make certain people uneasy. This very book, harmless jest though it is, might be banned in various locales, or even burned in others. Certain parents would claim *Howard the* (of all things) *Duck* capable of corrupting their children and advancing the cause of Satan in the modern world. Yes, that Satan.

The consequences would be dire.

Sales would suffer. The author, his agent, and their dependents would experience distress. The editor and her boss would become annoyed. Perfectly nice people in handsome, 'post-modern' offices in New York, Los Angeles and London would suffer depression, mood swing, loss of appetite, decreased productivity. Howard himself, when informed, would be livid. Even Satan would feel insulted – he has much bigger ducks to press than this measly paperback.

All of these are compelling reasons not to print the precise formulations and imprecations being formulated and imprecated by the bird and the fuzz trying to disrobe him. But they're not the right reasons.

For one thing, who gives a damn about the author or his agent? Who will lose a nanosecond's worth of sleep over the editor or her so-called boss? Who cares a fig for the mood, swinging or otherwise, of those people in their post-for-crying-out-loud-modern offices?

But the real reason for not including those s-words and f-words is (the cops are still grabbing all over Howard in an effort to remove a costume that he isn't actually wearing) that they're aesthetically inappropriate. With their appearance,

the overall tone and style of the 'text' would be marred.
Those words belong in some books – *Last Egg-Sit to Brook-lyn*, *Tropic of Flapricorn*, etc. – but not this one.

Besides the damage is done. You already know the words.
Bad things are already in everyone's vocabulary. Yes, yours
too. Still, if you absolutely must see them in print – if the
mere suggestion of three guys and a duck taking off somebody's clothes isn't compelling enough without talking dirty
– write them here:

'You   ,' Howard squawked.
'Hey, ya   ,' a cop squawked. 'Watch where ya put
your   ,   !'
'Oh,   it!' Kirby grabbed Howard's shirt.
'KWAAAK!' Howard yelped. 'That's my   , ya
stupid   !'
Finally, after a few more words (Hold him! . . . Let me go,
I'm a master of Quack – HeeeYAAAH! . . . Ow, get his arm!
. . . Take the jacket! . . . I've – OW! . . . NOT MY
SHORTS! . . . I can't find no zipper – I got it – OW! . . .
You're sick! Help! Police! . . . Ow! That's my arm, Hanson!
. . . Pull the head off! Pull the heh . . . Wait, stop, that's my
head . . . I'll pull your head off, copper! – Where's the – OW!
. . . Here! No. Oops. Sorry . . . I'll sue! HeeYA . . . I got the
shirt! . . . Police brutality! Ouch! Police bru . . . GOD
DAMN IT, KIRBY, WHERE'S THE ZIPPER ON THIS
THING?) the violence ebbed.
Lieutenant Weber had observed it all with the cool dis-
passion of a man patiently waiting for a hallucination to
disperse. Bev watched with a fist in her mouth, gnawing. At
last Kirby emerged from the fray, his own uniform a bit
mauled, and said, 'Uh . . . Lieutenant? There sort of is no
zipper. Sir.'
Beverly looked past him. Between the two other cops,
who were panting, stood Howard in his underwear. His
feathered chest was dishevelled but intact above his

shorts. His spindly little orange legs stuck out below.

Hanson added, 'No zipper and no Velcro, sir! I think his duckness is, like, inborn!'

'He appears to be an actual duck-type individual, sir,' Kirby said.

'If your goons are finished,' Howard said, 'I wanna ask the scientists when they're gonna send me home!'

'I'm going to talk to the scientists,' Weber said, tightly controlled. He looked at Howard. 'You're going to play sitting duck in jail, pal.' Weber told Hanson, 'Book him.'

'Uh . . . on what charge, sir?'

Weber thought a moment. 'Illegal alien.'

'You can't do that –!' Beverly said.

'It's done.' Weber walked out.

Two big cops handcuffed Howard and escorted him into the main lobby. Beverly, who had slipped away unseen, crept back through a side door as one of the cops went to fetch the car. The other discovered a small pack of cigars on a counter and helped himself. He lit up as he saw Bev.

'Sorry, miss, but you can't come in here.'

'Say,' Howard said, jumping atop a chair. 'I think I could use one of those.'

'Oh, really?' The cop held out the pack. Howard took one in his bound hands and popped it in his bill. Incredulous, the cop lit a match and held it out as Howard puffed the stogie to life. It was mediocre – not half as good as the brand he had outgrown back home, El Producto – but it would do. The cop, meanwhile, said, 'You mean ducks think? What do they think about?'

'Oh, you know,' Howard said. 'Money. Sex. Death. The usual.'

'No kiddin'?' The cop turned to Bev again. 'You'll have to leave, Miss. This is a restricted area.'

It was at that moment that Howard dropped his lit cigar into a trash bin full of perforated computer trimmings. As the cop moved to herd Beverly away Howard said loudly, 'Aw nuts! I dropped the cigar . . .'

The cop saw Howard rifling through the trash and hustled over, muttering, 'Great. Another fire while I'm on duty, that's all I need . . .' He reached the bin and bent over, digging around for the cigar. It was what Howard was waiting for.

He cried, 'So long, copper!', leapt high, and landed square on the cop's back. The police officer plunged head-first into the trash. Beverly ran over and nervously withdrew the cop's revolver. 'Hey –!' the man cried, but it was too late. The duck had the drop on him.

'Desperate ducks commit desperate acts,' Howard said. 'Let's have the keys, flatfoot.'

('Howard,' Beverly said after they'd uncuffed the duck and bolted from the building. 'Where'd you learn to talk like that?'

'Old TV shows,' he said. *Draked City. Mr Ducky. Peter Gull, Untouchabills*' etc. etc.)

They headed for the rear of the building. The plan was to hide in the shrubs until the cops assumed they'd escaped, then find Phil Blumburtt and figure out their next move. Police ran past them several times as they crouched. Then two cops met, barely a yard from where Howard and Bev held their breath.

'He's about two feet ten,' one told the other. 'Armed and dangerous.' (Howard tossed the police revolver onto the ground.) 'Better shoot to kill.'

'Right.' The cops dispersed.

'I know it's open season,' Howard said. 'But Jeez . . .'

The coast seemed clear. They stood up and made their way into a loading area. Its lights were out, probably short-circuited by the explosion, but strong floodlights trained on the building itself were burning brightly. It was then that they saw a single figure in silhouette against the floods, stalking towards them.

'Come on!' Beverly hissed.

'Forget it,' Howard said. 'If they're shooting to kill, I'm not playing clay pigeon.' To the approaching figure he called, 'Don't shoot! I give up!'

The figure – it wasn't in police uniform – abruptly shoved them behind some crates. Then he slumped against a wall and sank slowly to the ground, just as several police ran past without stopping. With the lights finally shining on the man and no longer in their eyes, Bev and Howard could discern his torn clothes, blackened face, bleary eyes, blasted expression. He looked vaguely familiar. Then Beverly gasped.

'It's Dr –'

'Der? What's "der" mean?'

'Doctor! It's Dr –'

'You mean –?'

'Howard – it's Dr Jenning!'

Ten

They recognized him from Carter's tape. The scientist could barely focus on Howard and Beverly; he seemed to be struggling with vast and terrible forces within himself. His body shook, his brow was damp, his breath came in gasps. He didn't look at all well.

Even after mastering his body Dr Jenning stared intently at the duck and his companion for almost a minute before he was able to speak. 'You . . . you must be the result of the first experiment.' Then he lost it again, clutching at his head and doubling over, groaning, retching, his system in turmoil. 'Oh my God . . .'

Howard turned to Beverly. 'Am I that ugly?'

'No . . .' Jenning made a visible effort to resist the pain that rippled through his system. 'It's not that. I'm burning up! It feels like my head is going to burst!' He sat up and took a deep breath. 'We were initiating functions on the laser spectroscope. And – it went out of control again. There was an explosion. I stumbled out here and must have passed out.'

Flashlight beams came dancing up towards them, slicing in tubular shafts through the lingering smoke in picturesque Spielbergian fashion. The fugitive trio sank further back into the shadows as several cops met nearby.

'See anything?' one asked. 'Mad scientist? Chick with nice legs? Duck from another planet?'

'Not today.'

'Keep looking.'

The cops moved on. Jenning said to Howard, 'Are they after you?'

Howard shrugged. 'They said "shoot to kill." I guess I take it kind of personally.'

The scientist nodded. 'I'm probably finished, too. These experiments were unauthorized. All this damage – not to mention whoever's been injured – or even killed! I'm responsible. My God . . .' He broke off and moaned, face contorted.

It was obvious they couldn't stay there. When Jenning had recovered from the latest onslaught of pain he led them to the car-park. They managed to dodge police surveillance until they came to his car. He settled into the driver's seat, and then hesitated, resting his head on the steering wheel. 'I'm starting to remember now . . . just before the explosion . . . I saw something come down! From space!'

'Maybe another duck!' Howard grew excited. 'Anyone I know?'

'It was horrible! Some grotesque, hideous shape of undefinable yet palpable evil!'

'My landlord!' Howard frowned as the scientist moaned and clutched his fevered brow. 'Doc, I think you suffered some kind of concussion or something.'

'No,' the scientist said hoarsely. 'I saw it. The laser brought you down the first time . . . This time, I'm afraid it's brought down some kind of monster . . . a . . . a representative and apologist for the worst kind of forces –'

'William F. Duckley, Junior!' Howard cried. 'Run!'

'Dr Jenning, we can talk about this later,' Beverly said. Her self-control was fraying. She motioned with her hands. 'Meanwhile let's start the car. Okay? Please?'

'But where will we go?' The scientist's voice was edged with panic. 'That evil is here now! And we've got no place to hide!'

'Fine,' Howard said. 'But let's have no place to hide somewhere else. Rev her up.'

He did, and they pulled out slowly towards the rear gate. It was closed and locked, with no guard in sight. Standing on the front seat between Beverly and Jenning, Howard yelled, 'Floor it!'

'The pain is spreading,' Jenning gasped. 'I don't know what I'm doing!'

'You're smashing through a gate! Let's go!'

Jenning grimaced and leaned on the gas; the car crashed through the chain link gate, sending its two halves flying.

(Back at the lab, Officer Hanson reported to Lieutenant Weber that a car of unknown drivership had crashed its way through the rear fence. Weber put out an APB on the vehicle, then reviewed various ways of instructing his forces to conduct a manhunt for a duck. He tested them out on Hanson. It didn't go too well; each of the five different wordings made Hanson laugh.)

Jenning, meanwhile, had increasing difficulty driving. They swerved along a road and swung erratically onto a highway, the poor man fighting the wheel at every turn. He cried, 'You've got to listen! I tell you – I saw it!'

'You're in shock, Doc,' Beverly said, her eyes on the road. She was waiting for things to settle down, but they wouldn't. 'You're imagining things from the explosion.'

'A great evil has landed!' He seemed to rock against the wheel, shifting the car from lane to lane. 'The world is in great danger!'

'It sure is when you're behind the wheel,' Howard said. 'We – WATCH IT!'

A car was heading right at them! And vice versa! Jenning jerked the wheel left and they swerved instantly into the wrong lane, set on a collision course directly into a succession of headlights. Howard seized the wheel and pulled hard, narrowly missing a giant semitrailer, which hurtled past with a piercing blast of its air horn. Jenning worked the pedals, clutching his stomach in agony as Howard steered. Actually it wasn't such a bad setup, as far as it went. But it couldn't go very far.

'You're gonna get us killed!' Howard observed.

'It feels like something – inside me! Gnawing at my guts!' Jenning gasped, and shut his eyes, nearly fainting. 'I can't hold out much longer. The pain – I feel like I'm transforming inside! Something's . . . growing inside me – replicating and taking over my internal organs. I can't control my own body –!'

'We'll stop at a rest room –' Beverly said.

'No . . .' His voice suddenly plunged into an urgent, harsh whisper. 'Howard . . . that monstrous shape . . . the one that I saw . . . It's inside me! That evil is in my body right now! The end of the world is coming . . . and I will cause it! My head – I – GAAAAAH!' In a paroxysm of pain, Jenning lurched once and passed out cold. He slumped onto the wheel, forcing it to the left. They were headed into oncoming traffic. Howard leapt into his lap and grabbed the wheel, struggling with it like a helmsman in a storm.

'Get his foot off the gas!' Bev yelled. 'Hit the brake! Look out –!'

They were plunging into an intersection, where a pickup truck was about to cross. Howard yanked the wheel and they swerved behind it. The car hit a soft shoulder and kept on going, out into thin air. Howard squawked. Beverly screamed. Jenning did nothing. The car flew – and slammed down onto an embankment, then rattled over a side road towards a café. Howard wrestled with the wheel, trying to shoulder the unconscious Jenning out of the way. The scientist's feet were still among the pedals, and Howard couldn't reach them.

'Bev!' he cried. 'The brake! Hit the brake!'

The car kept pounding towards the still-stationary restaurant. Beverly reached her feet in and stomped in blind panic at where the brake might be. Jenning's feet and ankles were like tree roots underfoot in a forest. Then she hit something firm but yielding, and stood on it for all she was worth. 'GOT IT!'

The car skidded, its rear swinging round in a fishtail spinout and throwing out a mighty cloud of dust. It kept skidding. The café, with its mammoth plate glass window, was rushing up at them at a stomach-churning speed. Bev was practically standing as Howard steered the skid. The car slowed, crossed the pavement, and rolled towards the café's giant picture window. They were five feet away and about to hit it –!

They did – the bumper kissed the window with a tentative tap, the expanse of glass quivered . . . and then held. No damage.

Beverly slumped back, drained. Howard breathed a heartfelt, 'Hoo-hah.' They looked at each other. Then they looked at Jenning.

He was smiling strangely. The mouth was grinning but the eyes were dead. It was the gracious zombie look of a society wife greeting a charity case. 'I'm dead,' Jenning remarked.

'We're all dead, pal,' Howard said. 'When the cops find us –'

'I am not Jenning any more.' The voice which uttered this was indeed nothing like the scientist's. It sounded eerie, mechanical, like a cross between one of those cut-and-paste phone company announcements telling you the number you are calling has been changed, and one of Dr Who's daleks. 'I am someone else now. I am [name not transliteratable into standard English], from [name, etc.].'

'Come on, he needs some coffee,' Bev said, opening her door.

'I do not desire coffee. I desire world domination.'

'That may not be on the menu,' Howard said and helped Jenning out of the car.

The restaurant was called Joe Roma's Cajun Sushi, a typical roadside joint with travellers installed in booths and locals slouching over the counter. A hostess bearing red leatheroid menus the size of rec room panelling greeted them with a frosty look. She regarded Howard for a moment, then said to Jenning, 'I'm sorry,' in a tone that suggested that, in reality, she wasn't sorry. 'We don't allow pets on the premises.'

Jenning stared at her, feverishly intense and utterly silent. Howard took his hand and led him past the hostess, saying, 'Seeing-eye duck.'

The hostess stared. Beverly smiled at her. 'He's just helpless without his duck. It's, like, real touching.'

They slid into a booth, Bev beside Howard, both facing the scientist or what was left of him. Howard, craning his neck in search of a waitress, did not see the following:

Jenning staring, as though hypnotized, at a glass of water.

Beverly smiling with amusement, and saying, 'What's the matter, haven't you ever seen water before?'

Jenning saying, 'No.'

Jenning holding out his hand and the glass sliding across the table into his grasp.

Beverly gaping.

Jenning gripping the glass and the water coming to an immediate galloping boil.

Beverly saying, 'Wow, you must have a major fever,' reaching across to place the back of her hand on his damp forehead, then jerking it away as though from a radiator.

Then the waitress arrived, a gum-cracking young lady with an easy manner and a fondness for children. 'Oh, wow,' she said, smiling at Howard. 'Your kid's costume is really radical. He must love it.'

'I'm very attached to it,' Howard said.

'Really.' She looked at Jenning, by now bathed in sweat and staring wide-eyed at her. To Howard she said, 'Your Dad's sort of into his own space. What do you think he'd like to eat?'

Jenning said, 'I no longer require human food.'

'Really,' she said. 'I know it's a drag, but you have to order something if you want to sit here.' Jenning continued to stare. To the waitress this was nothing new. Sometimes customers got weird, that's all. She coped with it by getting formal, creating a distance. She said, 'Would you like the special, sir?'

'You are about to witness the end of the old world and the beginning of the new!'

'That sounds real great,' she said. Then she whispered to Beverly, 'Is he, like, a TV evangelist or something?'

'We'll have three specials,' Bev said nervously. The waitress wrote it down and went off.

'Listen, Jenning,' Howard said. 'If you can tune back into reality for a second . . . I don't understand anything you're talking about. All I know is, I need that laser machine of yours to get me home. Is it still working?' The scientist did not speak. 'Hey, Jenning –'

'I told you,' the eerily mechanical voice said. 'I am not Jenning any longer. I am one of the Dark Overlords of the Universe.'

Howard looked at Beverly, perplexed. 'Is that some sort of lodge? My father used to belong to the Rotissararians –'

But Beverly was staring at Jenning, her stomach starting to churn. 'One of the what?'

'The Dark Overlords of the Universe. Tonight,' Jenning said, leaning forward, thrilled, 'your laser beam struck the Nexus of Sominus!'

Beverly frowned. 'I thought that was a sleeping pill.'

'It is not a sleeping pill,' Jenning said. Apparently possession by the alien entity had impaired his normally lively sense of irony. 'It is the place past all planets, the zone beyond zones. It is a region of demons.'

'Oh.'

'It is another dimensional plane!' Jenning's eyes widened, his voice taking on operatic grandeur. Actually he was overdoing it a little. 'It is that hated place of places to which we Dark Overlords were exiled aeons ago after losing the First Cosmic War.' He shrugged. 'It's also a planned community for energoids, which means it's just about the most boring place in the entire Continuum.'

*

The Nexus of Sominus: Condominium Dwellings for Today's
Lifeformstyle

Beauty. Elegance. Refinement. Luxury. Temperatures guaranteed to exceed 36,000,000°C. And the not in-considerable advantage of knowing that you have invested your affluence in a home-field force-structure unique in all the Three Extant Universes – and that its value is secure.

We commend to your ideational processing the Con-dominium home-field force-structures of the Nexus of Sominus, the only fully planned demon and quasi-material living development in the Known Grid.

Scrupulously designed to the smallest gluonic link, yet bold in vision and 'breath' taking in its macro-aspect, the Nexus of Sominus is located some 45 degrees Transverse/24 degrees Magnetic/31 degrees Absolute to the cosmically renowned Pulsar of a Thousand Oaks, mere parsecs from exciting, throbbing, imploding Netherzone Mall and Shop-ping Abyss. Convenient for all major trans-material generation units, the Nexus of Sominus offers the best of both Both-worlds: binary self-other energy exchange, and private precious-personal-moment maximization. Enter and behold an unparallelled universe of elegance, where the Mind-Body Problem is, quite simply, 'no problem'.

This, indeed, is your Place Within the Sun, where 'to Be or not to Be' is literally beside the point. Topologically unique access-zones, coded to your private decay rate, assure absolute security for your 'self' and your beloved physical manifestations. Award-winning materialization experts have provided a host of semi-real environment-simulacra that give new meaning to the word 'visible'.

Moreover, each unit is utterly unique, both in spatial layout and temporal duration. Graviton-power assures that each floor, regardless of external phenomena, will remain a floor. Every sub-sector is accessible to one or more wavelengths of the Electromagnetic Spectrum-standard of impression-transmission since one ten-billionth of a second after the Big Bang itself. Cable-ready leisure field? Of course. Anti-matter nourishment poles? Standard. Tile bathrooms? 'Naturally.'

And your neighbours? A cosmological blend of demons, pseudos, quasimorphs and energoids, all of 'whom' share – with you – the highest standards for dwelling-stasis and thought-form transmissibility.

Yet the Nexus of Sominus is more than just another randomly fluctuating gauge-field of localized Condominium events. You will find within its magnetic boundaries a complete, self-sustaining eco-matrix. A fully accredited, Continuum-authorized Educational Loop provides complete schooling for nascent forms, from Inchoate to Pre-Stable to grade K-445.

Step-up transformer centres – reserved for the exclusive use of Nexus residents, of course – offer the ultimate in convenience for those who, possessing 'bodies', desire to exercise them. Solar windsurfing, three Olympus-sized swarming pools (indoor, outdoor, coexistent-with-door) and a professionally designed eighteen-black-hole championship golf course attest to the level of luxury that has made the Nexus of Sominus the first choice among 'today's' most discerning, whether for principal residences, or pseudopieds-à-terre.

That many of the most prestigious concerns from the Fortune Five Trillion have selected the Nexus of Sominus as the site of their discorporate headquarters merely provides additional lustre to its already glittering list of residents.

May we add your thought-frequency as well?

NOTE: This does not constitute an offer of sale, nor does this sentence constitute a disclaimer. The Nexus of Sominus does not exist, nor is the preceding clause a true statement. Complete offering terms are available in a Prospectus via Guild-monitored Thought-link with the Sponsor. Contact, on a minimum of three standard wavelengths, the Nexus of Sominus Partnership, 1 The Singularity, Centre of Maximum Entropy, Edge of Unimagineable Chaos, 11215.

'So you're a bunch of old war vets?' Howard asked.

'Well,' Jenning smiled. 'Because we exist outside Time our age is meaningless. We think of ourselves as a street gang.' His eyes grew wide, his expression feverish. 'We neutron-bomb up and down the wavelengths of the Nexus and do a prime number on the squares and cubes! It's a gas! Totally plasmatic!'

'Howard,' Bev said softly. 'I think this man is very, very sick.'

Jenning let his hand drop onto the table like a felled tree, its rigid index finger pointing at Howard. 'You. The Duck. Just as you were brought down accidentally, tonight the laser beam released me from that region of white-bread tedium, and pulled me down into that laboratory.'

'My, my . . .'

'During the explosion, I entered the scientist Jenning's body.' The creature leaned forward and said to Howard, chatty and confidential, one extraterrestrial to another, 'So, I have disguised my true form, which would be considered hideous and revolting to these beings. I suggest you think about doing the same. Believe me, it's worth it. It pays for itself in basic energy metabolizing alone.'

Then the waitress returned. She set three plates in front of them and stood back, smiling. 'Anything else I can get everybody?'

Howard recoiled in horror and cried, 'EeeeYAAAH! WHAT IS THIS?'

'You ordered three specials,' she said. 'Is something wrong?'

Jenning said to her, 'This will mean the extinction of all existing life-forms!'

'Gee,' she said, 'you haven't even tasted it yet.'

'Whattaya think, I'm some kind of cannibal?' Howard gasped.

'Hey.' The waitress wasn't sure whether she was being put on by snotty college types or dealing with actual weirdos. 'Now look. You ordered three Huevos Rancheros. So here they are. What's –'

'Eggs!' Howard snarled. 'I don't eat eggs! I'm a duck, you idiot! Get rid of 'em!'

'Jeez, sorry. Try reading the menu next time or something.' She picked up the plates and walked off.

'I can't believe this planet!' Howard said. 'Fried eggs!' He shivered.

Jenning, meanwhile, was glaring at bottles of ketchup and mustard on the table. 'Edible foods in primary colours. Interesting.'

Beverly watched, fascinated, as a beam of light shot out from his eyes and hit the hapless condiments. 'Uh, Howard . . .?' The bottles began to vibrate. Suddenly they exploded, sending a thick splash of red and yellow across the table top.

'Hey, how'd you do that –?' Howard said.

'Look out!' Bev pointed. 'He's got something in his pocket!'

They cringed – but Jenning merely extracted a plastic circuit card, which he placed reverently on the table amid the red and yellow ooze.

'This is the code-key,' he said solemnly. 'This activates the laser spectroscope. I will use it when I direct the laser beam into the Nexus of Sominus again – when I bring down the other Dark Overlords!'

Howard snatched at the card. 'Stand in line, pal! I got dibs on the laser first. This code-key's my ticket home!' As soon as Howard took the card, small sparks and rays flared off Jenning's fingers. 'Jeez, look at his hand!'

'That's nothing,' Bev said. 'Look at his face!'

Jenning's face had gone deathly pale, his eyes suddenly darker, his features more gaunt and contorted. He spoke. It sounded raspy, inhuman, worse even than Joan Rivers on *The Tonight Show* calling the president's wife 'a truly classy lady'. (To applause yet.)

'Soon the Dark Overlords will engulf the world!' Jenning intoned. 'Nothing human will remain here!'

'Yeah? Well, nothing duck's going to remain here either. Let's go, Bev.' Howard seized Beverly's hand and said to Jenning, 'Hate to eat and run –'

They couldn't get out. Their way was blocked, not by Dark Overlords seeking to exterminate all human life in the universe, but by something almost as bad: three grinning truckers in green mesh gimme caps. They were looking for trouble in all the wrong places.

'Hey, lookit,' said one. 'A talking duck!'

'Am-skray, uster-Bay,' Howard said. 'Beat it.'

'Lord,' another one giggled. 'What is *that*?'

The third said, 'You jackass. This guy's a ventriloquist. And the duck is his dummy. Go on, say something, dummy.'

'You might not wanna hear what I say, stupid,' Howard snarled.

The trucker was not amused. In fact he grabbed Jenning by the front of his jacket and said, 'Hey. You make him say that, jerkoff?'

'Leave him alone!' Bev cried. 'He's been the victim of an industrial mishap!'

The first trucker laughed. 'Yeah? What's this one's excuse?' He pointed to Howard. 'Must be some kinda Farm School mutation. I hear they're tryna develop chickens with four legs –'

'Make tracks!' Howard said. 'Hit the road, cowboy!'

'Hey –' The second trucker suddenly seized Howard and picked him up. He plucked the code-key out of the hapless duck's hand and examined it closely. 'What's this? Some kinda duck credit card?'

'Maybe it's the key to his duckmobile,' the first one chuckled.

116

'Give me that, or you're gonna be sorry!'

'You'd better watch it,' Beverly said. 'He's a Master of Quack Fu.'

'Yeah?' The trucker with the code key slipped it into his pocket and with a leer drew back a fist and said to Howard, 'I'll Quack Fu you, birdbrain –'

WHOMP! No, not the 'whomp' of the trucker's meaty fist in our duck's much-abused face. But the tiny, contained 'whomp' of Howard's two fingers in the trucker's eyes! A Three Stoogesesque demonstration of speed and finesse! The big lug hollered and Howard proceeded to bite his godalmighty nose! He dropped the bird and grabbed at his own ailing face.

'Come on, Bev! Run!'

But the third trucker blocked Beverly's way. He reached in a Howardly direction. 'I think we better squash this thing before it does any more damage –'

The bird skipped away, onto a stool and from there onto the counter. The truckers gave chase. Other locals backed off, cheered, cursed, stared, punched each other. Anything for some excitement. Howard hotfooted it across the counter, high-stepping in several dinners along the way. Some of them were hot – meat loaves, chicken halves, roast beefs, etc. Some were cold – healthy salads, local fruit plates, ice cream sundaes. The contrast, on Howard's sensitive webbed feet, was revivifying. It was to a Swedish spa as miniature golf is to real golf.

Beverly, meanwhile, leapt from the booth and tried to reach him. But she was crowded out. She almost didn't see, therefore, Howard seize a pie (coconut custard, probably) and fling it into a trucker's face. He grabbed more items – sandwiches, a plate of fries, a platter of doughnuts – and hurled them at his pursuers.

It was every duck's (and person's) food fight fantasy of a lifetime – but as a holding action against aggressors it wasn't working. Howard remained a single duck, while the number of people chasing him mounted steadily. They now included other customers, conservative types who objected to their dinners being snatched from beneath their chins and thrown at people to whom they had not been properly introduced.

Beverly ran back to the booth and appealed to the waitress, who was calmly clearing the table. 'Please! Call the police! They're going to hurt him!'

Jenning looked even paler than before, his eyes darker, his voice an *Exorcist*-worthy rasp. Whatever was renting his body was proving an undesirable tenant. 'An evil unlike any you can imagine is about to engulf the world!' he intoned to the waitress.

She shrugged. 'Nah. We have fights in here all the time.'

Howard, meanwhile, found himself hooked onto an order-slip carousel at the cook's window, spinning around in a furious little circle as a dozen people closed in. Someone grabbed the wheel – and Howard shot off, airborne, and landed on a waiter's trolley, which rolled down the aisle. The mob roared and swarmed after him. As he rolled past their booth, Howard spied the scientist and cried, 'Jenning! I could use a hand here, if you're not too busy –!'

The rest was drowned out by a mighty crash of dishes as Howard's trolley smashed into another one, fully laden. Jenning barely raised his eyes – until, that is, a truck pulled up outside, its headlights momentarily flaring in through the window. This prompted Jenning to wheel towards it and, with a glare that brought an unearthly glow to his very eyes, shatter the headlights in an explosion of glass.

Meanwhile, they had Howard.

'We're gonna cook this sucker's goose!' a trucker shouted.

'Pluck him!' cried a customer.

Others joined in. 'Stuff him!'

'Bake him!'

'Roast him!'

'Shove him in the microwave!'

'Preheat oven to moderate (350°F)! Rub his skin with half

a lemon! Sprinkle his inside with salt and pepper! Place him on a rack in a roasting pan and roast, without basting, about twelve minutes per pound, or longer if desired! Fifteen minutes before he's done, sprinkle his outside with salt and pepper! If desired, before roasting, fill his cavity with any desired stuffing! Roast him, stuffed, at approximately fifteen minutes per pound!'

'Yeah, and serve him with wild rice, a green salad and a hearty, robust red wine!'

The place was crawling with gourmets. By the time they had Howard pinned to the counter, twelve different recipes had been shouted, rejected, combined, dismissed. With fruity vinegars. With chestnuts. Peking-style, to be hung from the neck until done. Should they tie him up? Was he trussworthy? There was much spirited debate.

Then the Chinese chef who worked in the back emerged, a giant cleaver gleaming in his expert hands. He did not lack for bulging biceps. Even happy-go-ducky H. began to worry.

'Lord love a duck!' he groaned. 'Is this the end of Howard?'

Eleven

The crowd converged on Howard the Duck in a frenzy of gourmet excitement. Small wonder. There is nothing more American than getting a bunch of folks together at the local roadhouse, tanking them up on a couple-twelve beers, and turning 'em loose on a three-foot duck from outer space. There is something in the American soul that hankers for fresh poultry – and doesn't mind marshalling the manpower and the hardware to get it.

Ask the Colonel – 'The Man Who Made Eleven Herbs and Spices Famous, Albeit In Secret'. Ask Frank Purdue – 'The Man Who Resembles New York City Mayor Ed Koch, Who In Turn Resembles A Chicken'. Ask Howard the Duck – 'The Man Who Is Not So Much A Man As He is A Duck'.

But other forces were at work in this group's enthusiasm to grab, truss, and roast the hapless fowl. For this was a collection of Americans as contemporary as now, eager to participate in the gastronomic revolution sweeping the nation. Howard's last words, before being dragged out of sight, were terse and economical. Addressing the individual in the booth (whose eyes had begun to flare slightly and emit more sparks than is customary for a person), he cried, 'Jenning! Don't just sit there! This is serious! They're gonna cook me!' Yet what he surely meant was something like this:

'Jenning! Don't just sit there! This is serious – yet it also partakes in the new-found spirit of experimentation, innovation, discovery and sheer fun that has informed American cuisine for the past fifteen years or so! They're gonna cook me – and they're gonna make use of scrupulously fresh, seasonally available ingredients! They're gonna be unafraid to apply a liberally eclectic hand in their use of spices, herbs and ingredients hitherto reserved for more traditionally 'foreign' dishes. Jenning, I'm thinking of such Oriental things as soy sauce, fresh ginger, tofu, and tree-ear mushrooms. And of such Italian ingredients as fresh pasta, the tomato puree known as 'passata,' and virgin olive oil. They're gonna cook me, yes – but it may be in one of any number of ways, from spit-roasting over mesquite wood to boning, marinating and charcoal grilling. They may, Jenning, process my meat into dense, highly-spiced sausages, to be strewn upon a small, extravagantly fresh pizza with three kinds of cheeses! They may serve me in a more familiar oven-roasted manner – yet accompany me with any of a wide range of currently popular vegetable preparations. Think of it, Jenning! Purees of leeks, squash, fennel or spinach! Stir-fried broccoli, peppers, snow peas or little teeny-tiny, eenie-weeny, itty-bitty, microgoddamscopic baby zucchini! Yes, Jenning, they're gonna cook me – but what an honour, to be stuffed with corn bread and wild mushrooms, as was once prepared by Alice Waters and her inspired staff at San Francisco's esteemed Chez Panisse! As the recipe says, Jenning: "Remove the head, neck and feet from the duck and be sure to leave enough neck skin to cover a little stuffing." Jesus Christ, Jenning, what am I saying? HELP!'

Beverly watched in dismay as the mob bore the bird into the back. She turned to the somewhat deranged scientist. 'Listen! Please help him! If you want to destroy the world, fine.' It was a major concession. Conceivably she was not authorized to make it. 'But Howard's not a part of it! You've got to do something!'

Jenning did something. He stared dully ahead.

In the kitchen, meanwhile, they had Howard on a chopping block. When one faction began to tie his legs together, argument flared. Traditionalists swore that trussing assured 'a jucier bird', progressives called that a myth and held that binding the legs was unnecessary. Howard took advantage of the debate to yell, 'JENNING! You're missing this! They're seasoning me!' He pleaded with the chef and the rowdy customers, 'Wait! You better knock it off! You don't want to get my friend angry –!'

'Oh yeah?' one of the truckers sneered. 'Why not?'

'Because he's one of the Dark Overlords of the Universe!'

Immediately the crowd became silent. They stared at the duck. Howard plunged on, 'And he can destroy you!' There was utter quiet. 'And this café!' A woman gasped. 'And all of Earth!' Absolute stillness pervaded the kitchen. Howard concluded, in a dramatic whisper, 'And . . . everything!'

It was then that they all started laughing their heads off. Howard shrugged. 'Yeah, well, I didn't buy it either, at first – Yikes!'

The chef had touched Howard's neck with the blade, to zero-in. At least, Howard thought, it was sharp. It wouldn't hurt too much. Then the man raised it high, preparing for the decisive chop. 'Jenning! I think they mean it –' Howard stopped, his eye caught by some activity he could just barely see through the open kitchen door – activity back at the booth. 'Uh – oh,' he said. 'He's getting up! I warned you –'

Jenning had in fact begun to stand slowly. The lynch, or roast – or whatever their desired form of preparation would ultimately be – mob turned as one and laughed at the sight.

'What happened?' one of the truckers guffawed. 'His quaaludes wear off?'

Bev, though, recoiled in her seat. A heartfelt, 'Oh, my God,' escaped her lips. She had just seen what the others could not – yet. What she saw looked something like this:

Jenning's transformation was complete. A luminescent aura of cold light and humming energy now enveloped his body. His hair glowed. His eyes flared, emitting sparks and rays as if a raging bioelectric fire possessed him. If an electric bug zapper were to attain human form it would look like this. If a scary-but-harmless Van de Graaf generator (those globes on top of columns seen in so many 50's science fiction mad-scientist movie labs, giving off lightning-like strings of electricity) were to become man, this is the guy like whom it would look.

The café went strangely silent. The chef, cleaver raised, froze. The crowd of Howard's tormentors all stared in something like horror at the sight of Jenning, a lumbering human form swathed in sizzling electrical energy, rising from his hitherto innocent booth.

'It's like somethin' out of a nightmare!' a trucker whispered, his sturdy teamster's soul stirred to poetry.

'He musta eaten the chilli,' ventured a waiter.

As for Howard, he sat up partially and muttered, 'Jeez. He really *is* one of the Dark Overlords of the Universe.'

Jenning spoke. Or, rather, it spoke. Its voice – eerie, mechanical, commanding, unearthly – struck Howard's shell-like organs of sound as being unlike anything ever heard by duck ear since the beginning of Time, or at least since the climactic 'Are-you-a-god?' scene of the ostcom (ostensible comedy) film, *Goosebusters*. 'Release the bird.'

Several customers gulped. What had begun for them as a routine evening's cheeseburger deluxe had become *a confrontation with Ultimate Evil*.

'HOWARD.'

'Uh – me?' Imagine the duck's excitement. Which of us has not yearned to be on a first-name basis with an embodiment of sheer malevolence?

'You. Bring me the code-key.'

'I'm sorta tied up, Jen –'

'Not funny. Release him.'

'You heard him, guys!' Howard called to the staring crowd. 'Release him. I'm him. So, uh, why don't you just release me and we'll call it quits. Can't keep a Dark Overlord of the Universe waiting. They get cranky and then –' He gave a don't - mind - me - I'm - just - a - schmendrick - trying - to - get - along - in - a - world - largely - populated - by - people - bigger - smarter - and - braver - than - I - am - but - still - I -

may - know - one - or - two - things kind of grin. '– It takes three hundred years to get 'em to go back to sleep . . .'

'Ah, I never heard such bull pucky,' one trucker said. He was not an individual about whom it could be said, that he was alive to nuance. He grabbed the cleaver from the chef and started towards Jenning. 'C'mere, pal.'

'I am not a pal.' The creature raised its hand and pointed.

The cleaver shot out of the trucker's hand and flew, end over end, towards the assembled customers. It swooped! As one, they ducked, as one duck did as they did. THUD! went the cleaver, biting deep into the chopping block and severing Howard's bonds.

The bird leaped up. 'Sorry, guys, but 86, the roast duck –'

Jenning gestured with his hand, and growled. The gas jets at the stove shot up ten feet in a roaring forest of blue flame. He swept his hand in a maitre d'-like fashion, sending a cyclone of sheer force whipping through the café. There was the Dolby-pure sound of a furious whirlwind as dishes, napkins, glasses, silverware, Danishes, muffins both bran and corn, fries both French and home – in a word, anything not nailed down – went flying. Did somebody say 'food fight'? Here was food holocaust.

In the kitchen, the assembled throng abandoned thoughts of duck dinners and ran for their lives.

Kitchens are narrow places, hardly designed for the staging of group stampedes. Howard had to shoulder and elbow his way among the scattering humans at great cost, bruise-wise, to where the trucker who'd hoisted the cleaver had fallen, in a stupor, to the floor.

'I warned you,' the bird said. 'He has a temper.' He snatched the code-key from the dazed man's pocket and made his way out into the main room. 'I got –!'

He was brought up short by the sight of the bartender emerging from behind the bar, a baseball bat in his fist and a look of pugnacious outrage on his face. Here, at last, was a man who knew his way around a restaurant brawl. He could

124

dish it out. He could take it. Maybe he was Joe Roma himself. 'Come on!' he spat. 'Let's get this guy!'

'Yeah!' somebody snarled. A few others grabbed what weapons they could – a basket of rolls, a napkin dispenser. Things like that. They closed ranks behind the man with the bat, and the small posse advanced, sneering. But the soda hoses behind the bar reared up like snakes, and began spraying them with various refreshing beverages! The TV above the bar came on, and flipped madly through its repertoire of channels. And then the TV, as though itself disgusted with the unremitting junk on the networks and the locals, blew the hell up!

The creature 'Jenning' glared and a line of glasses along a counter shattered. Bottles of liquor, arrayed behind the bar like buildings in a skyline against the mirror, suddenly leapt up and flew at the advancing bartender and his cohorts, pelting them with glass and showering them with booze. They cursed, they hit the dirt, they dived under tables, they cowered and stared in awe. Another trucker took the chain off the hostess's barricade and began to swing it, slowly, menacingly, like a bolo knife. Jenning's eyes flared and sent the man reeling back, stunned by a gust of wind that slammed him into a wall.

Howard reached Beverly. 'I got the code-key!'

'Let's get out of here!'

The third trucker charged Jenning, a chair raised over his head. The creature despatched him with a pointed finger, sending the man flying backwards through a window and out into the night. Howard and Bev made for the front door – which slammed shut in their faces. Chairs and planters, as though on wheels, slid in front of them, blocking their exit and reminding everybody of the battle scene at the climax of *Macbeth*. Bev and Howard, trapped, looked at Jenning and wondered if he would destroy them utterly with the merest exercise of his indomitable will, or what.

'You will not leave.'

'Well,' Howard said, 'If you ins – KWAAAK!' Something had grabbed at him and dragged him backwards across the floor, an invisible force that he could not pinpoint nor resist. It was an uncanny sensation. So was what happened next: Howard found himself lifted into the air – where he remained, poised six feet up, without visible means of support.

'Howard,' Beverly said. 'Get down!'

'Sure,' remarked the agreeable duck. 'How?'

Jenning came forward. His eyes were red. His head glowed yellow. Blue flame-like wisps played around his body. He looked like a gravely sick man. For a Dark Overlord, though, he looked damn good. 'Give me the code-key.'

'Oh yeah?' Howard mustered some of the old spunk. 'What if I don't . . .?' He smiled. 'Little joke –'

'Do not provoke me.'

Jenning glared. Beverly screamed. The duck rose straight up and banged his head on the ceiling, turned over, and squawked, 'Gaah! Jeez, you broke my head!'

The code-key fell out of Howard's hand onto a table. For Jenning to open a glowing, radiant hand and impel the card to lift, by itself, and float into his grasp, was but the work of a moment.

'I will now summon the other Dark Overlords.'

'Hey!' Howard yelled, still aloft. 'What about me? I got better things to do than hang around here all day!'

With a glare Jenning brought Howard down. Hard. The duck spun, shuddered, and crashed into the table, breaking it. Beverly rushed over to him, Jenning moved towards them and reached for her. She screamed.

His fingers burned their imprint into her arm. Smoke came forth. He dragged her past Howard, who looked up groggily and tried to focus on what was happening. What was happening was, the creature was shoving Beverly out of the door.

'Bev!' He managed to come to his webbed feet and ran out,

leaving behind him the smoking, blasted ruins of a totally destroyed Italo-Cajun/Creole-Japanese café.

Outside, Jenning forced Beverly into the detached cab of a giant diesel truck. Her struggles were completely useless – he had the strength of a machine. Her arm was killing her, although he seemed to have modulated his heat so that her flesh no longer actually burned. Beverly knew he could kill her with a look. Her heart was in her throat. She could do little more than sit in the passenger seat as Jenning revved the giant engine to life.

'Beverly!'

It was Howard, running out of the café. He was caught in the glare of the truck's headlights. Jenning had thrown the cab into gear and was bearing down on the tiny bird. She cried, 'No! Look out!'

Jenning grinned and leaned on the gas.

Howard squawked and hit the dirt. As the huge truck roared at him, Howard threw himself on his knees and covered his head and waited for the end of the world, exactly as he'd been taught in third grade during those useless air raid drills, back when the authorities believed (or claimed to believe) that all you had to do to survive an atomic blast was 'duck . . . and cover'. In that split-second of paralytic fear, he remembered it well . . .

An announcement would come over the P.A. system – itself an event in the middle of the day, with the school's leaden-voiced principal intoning, 'Teachers please prepare for the civil defence drill.' The P.A. speaker was a mesh-faced box mounted up on the wall above the front blackboard (which was green, itself a disturbing paradox). It was not quite a radio and not exactly a person. Howard would watch the speaker, hear the voice and feel his mind turn to Turkish taffy as he failed to understand what was going on.

The drill would commence with the thrilling, terrifying whoop of the air raid siren. Even Howard, at age ten, sensed that such an insistent, unmusical noise could only signal danger. He loved it. Then the class would stand, and leave the room in single file – 'in single file' became a phrase with magical properties. Every group action of the class, from trudging on field trips to going to the gym for 'assemblies' to shuffling to the library, was commenced 'in single file'.

In this case, the destination of the single file was the hall. This struck Howard as absurd. Getting into single file to go into the hall was like getting all dressed up to sit in the car. By the time the single file had snaked out into the hall, Howard was thoroughly disorientated.

The teacher would distribute Howard and his fellow duck-lings along the wall, facing the lockers. Then the youngsters would fall to their knees, and bend over, clasping their hands behind their heads and cover their ears with their elbows. Thus genuflecting to the god 'Civil Defence', they would wait, knees cold on the floor, heads dizzying as they filled with blood, foreheads on their thighs. After a period of time, during which nothing happened, they would be told to rise. They would return to the room in single file.

Howard had no clear notion of why they did this. It was never explained to them – it was simply described as 'an air raid drill'. Later, when he was older and saw documentaries and movies about Duck World War II, he learned what 'air raid' meant. In retrospect he conjured the image of a squadron of bombers over his town, dropping strings of wobbly atomic bombs, while he and his classmates knelt in the halls. No wonder ducks grew up believing that there were unexplained things one simply had to do in life, regardless of how baffling or meaningless they seemed.

Howard hated the part of himself that had always ducked and covered without asking questions. Okay, so he'd been ten. Still. There was a good-duck part of his character that did as it was told, trusting in the expertise and good intentions of whoever was doing the telling – a teacher, a boss, a cop, a salesman, a maitre d' – anyone with authority.

He had always had to force himself to ask the necessary questions. Had he put his webbed foot down early, in third grade, and said, 'Why are we doing this?' he might have cultivated a more independent spirit. He might have grown up with the relaxed ease others seemed to have when stopped for a traffic ticket or pressurized to buy something in a store. He wouldn't have had to learn to be irascible. Had he gone through life with his mental legs untrussed, he'd have grown up a juicer bird.

a flash, at the same time he glimpsed the maniacal face of Jenning at the big, almost horizontal steering wheel in the cab. And as he bunched himself into a tight ball of feathers and fear, he had one more brilliant insight: as the third grade ducklings had been to their teacher – passive, trusting, unquestioning dupes – so had the teacher been to the principal, and the principal to the Civil Defence Agency. Who knew how high that chain of command extended, with everyone trusting the authority figure above them, as the ducklings tucked themselves into a ball on the floor and waited for disaster?

The vehicle thundered over him, tyres to either side, spewing gravel and digging parallel gullies as it went. He felt the wind stirred up by its passing and had a moment's awareness of his own continuing thought. So he wasn't dead.

Slowly, his head reeling and his body a single throbbing welt, Howard struggled to his feet. He had learned something! He had had an insight.

First, for one thing, he would no longer be so passive and accepting. He would act.

'Gotta make a plan,' he thought. 'Gotta save Bev.' He needed a clear scheme. He needed to know what to do, and when to do it. He paced furiously in a circle and spoke aloud.

'Yeah. Okay. First. Can't do it alone.' Good start. Sensible. 'I got it! I'll get help!' He was pleased. It was a fantastic idea. He'd get help. But then what?

The answer came in a flash of insight: *he'd do something*!

Things were falling smartly into place now. First he'd get help, and then, with the assistance of the help, he'd do something. It struck him as a profoundly intelligent strategy. Howard felt a renewed sense of confidence, a rousing return of his customary physical vigour. His energy was coming back. His mind was clearing. His feathers felt fluffier than they had in ages. Most importantly, his spirit was reviving.

He knew there had to be a way to stop Jenning, save Beverly, and make his way back to his own world – and he was determined to find it. Nothing could stop him now. He was crafty, resolute, and utterly unshakeable. He hadn't asked for this, hadn't asked to be here among hairless apes or featherless bipeds or Dark Overlords, or whatever these creatures were. It wasn't his fault he was trapped in a world he never made. The sooner he marshalled his forces and took action, the sooner he'd rescue Bev, who was the only creature he could think of who meant anything to him.

Satisfied that he had put everything in order, Howard the Duck said, 'Okay! Let's go!' and passed out.

Twelve

They were barrelling down the highway at seventy miles per hour, Jenning glaring out the windshield and giving off random sparks. Beverly turned towards him, her eyes twisted in horror, her mouth wide in rage. Actually it may have been the other way around. 'You killed him!' she screamed. 'You killed Howard!'

Jenning glanced at her with glacial indifference. He was as moved by her accusation as a Hollywood film producer by a screenwriter's protests. Less, if that's possible. (It isn't.) Then he glared at her with those fiery eyes, and emitted a gaseous snarl. 'I need your body.'

'You slime!' she said – and she meant it to sting. 'I've heard that one before!'

'The Dark Overlords cannot exist on this planet,' he explained, 'unless they grow inside a human body.'

Beverly gulped and sat back, as far away from the monster as she could get without actually falling out of the cab. Perhaps that may have been preferable to staying there, but the speed they were going made it too chancy. She looked out the window at the passing landscape.

She had wanted a life out of the ordinary, and it had arrived with a vengeance. Fay Wray once felt as she now felt. And, for that matter, Jessica Lange. Who else? Let's see . . . Carrie Fisher in *Jedi*, maybe. Sigourney Weaver in *Alien*. What the hell kind of name was Sigourney, anyway? Hadn't Bev read somewhere that her real first name was sort of plain, that she'd changed it to Sigourney? What did you call someone with a name like that? 'Siggy?' 'Goor?' It was like what's her name, Tovah Feldshuh. Her real name was Terry, for Chrissake. Maybe Beverly should move to Hollywood and change her name. Was Sigourney Switzler too dumb? Oh, sure, people would say. You stole it from Sigourney Weaver. Tough. Let 'em. Nobody complained when Diane Keaton changed her name from whatever it was. Or when Audrey Hepburn showed up with Katherine Hepburn's last name. How can there be two movie stars named Hepburn? Has anybody ever even *heard* of anyone named Hepburn in real life? Or Keaton, for that matter? What are the odds on two movie stars having names like that? In fact, come to think of it, how could there actually be a guy named Armand Hammer? Was that supposed to be some kind of amazing coincidence, that an oil millionaire was named after a box of baking soda? Were his parents kidding, or what –

'What am I thinking about!' Beverly screamed. The heat and energy radiated by Jenning's body must have altered the air in the cab; she had been slipping into the sort of fanciful mind-meanderings that normally preceded either sleep or asphyxiation. She rolled down the window and drew deeply on the cool night air.

With her head out the window, she did not see Jenning's own head tip down towards the steering wheel, as though he were falling asleep.

The truck swerved right, onto the shoulder, losing traction and throwing out a little spray of gravel. It looked to Bev as though Jenning had passed out. She screamed. He jerked awake, and steered the cab back onto the highway.

'Tired,' he said, almost chattily. 'Need energy.'

He flicked on the radio and got some dumb rock song. The lyrics were either, 'Come on, baby, let's party,' or 'Come on, party, let's baby.' He spun the dial.

'– in the middle of a Tooooooooooooooo MUCH MUSIC . . . MARATHON on Dubbayew Kay . . . Zee! Zee! CHOONG! KA-CHOONG CHOONG!) andnow-let'sgotonumber – SEVEN – onthekwazeeWKZZ-TopTwentyhere's . . . PAT BENatar . . . LOVE . . . is like World War Three –'

'– okesman told reporters that when the President said "It's a known fact that taxes cause cancer," he had misspo –'

'– of the NCAA's Board of Collegiate Athletic Standards said he was opposed to mandatory drug testing for college athletes on Constitutional grounds, citing the First and Fourth Amendments. He did, however, state that he had no opposition to drug pop-quizzing –'

'– I like the way you cross the street, 'cause you're Prehhhhh-shussssss –'

'– ifty THOUSAND dollars – and that winner could be you. Just write your name on a piece of paper, and throw it away. That's all. Then send five dol –'

'– Singin 'bout . . . the same old boys –
Same old problems, same old noise
Tired a' home, an' there's . . . nowhere ta run . . .
Music's business . . . ain't no fun . . .
(And I'm)
Bored . . . in the You-Ess . . . Ey . . .'

Jenning turned it off with a snort. 'More Energy!' He opened the glove compartment, found nothing of use inside and slammed it shut.

Then he spied the cigarette lighter.

He withdrew the lighter and examined it closely. Then he threw it out the window. Horrified, Beverly could still not help watching – and had an excellent view, therefore, when Jenning's mouth opened wide, and a tentacle-like tongue writhed out of it, wriggled through the air, and plunged into the lighter base in the dashboard. There it remained, three feet long, throbbing. Jenning drove, eyes ahead, as the hideous organ drew on the engine's electrical power.

'Jeez I'm gonna puke!' Beverly moaned. 'Oh, God, that's the grossest thing I ever saw!' A shudder rippled through her, but she found it irresistible to sneak quick peeks at the gently pulsing tongue.

And the truck cab roared through the night towards some kind of terrible fateful destiny.

Meanwhile, back at Joe Roma's Cajun Sushi, fire fighters pulled wreckage away from the charred, smouldering, dripping ruins. The car-park swarmed with vehicles with flashing roof lights – cops, ambulances, fire engines, reporters, TV crews, and urgent, hustling teams of paramedics, para-legals, para-police and para-firemen. Red lights flashed; amber lights whirled. The scene was festive and macabre all at the same time.

Also on hand, pointing in wonder and shielding their children on cue, was a crack squad of para-bystanders. Their job: to gather in a cluster and look appalled or fascinated whenever ordinary bystanders were unavailable. At remote locations. In inclement weather. Whenever a public event required an innocent group of observers and secondary victims, the para-bystanders were there. It is to them, in sincere appreciation of their dedication and skill in the cause of bystanding, that parts of this book are gratefully dedicated.

Lieutenant Weber was also on the scene. He had proceeded there directly from the Aerodyne mess. A destroyed hush-hush research lab, and now this. Normally, of course, a bar-room brawl or a restaurant fire was nothing unusual. He wouldn't even have had to come – the uniforms could handle it. But the eyewitness accounts of how this place had been wrecked were absolutely wacko.

'At first I thought it was this kid in a duck suit,' the waitress told one of Weber's men. 'But then I like remembered? That Halloween was like last year? So it was this anomaly.'

Then another cop called Weber over to hear the report of a man in bandages, who was accompanied by his gleeful kid. 'This guy musta been eight feet tall,' the man said. 'He had ray guns shooting out of his eyes and he was blowin' the entire place to smithereens.'

'Yeah!' the kid piped. 'It was great!'

Weber shook his head. If this had a connection with the Aerodyne business, it wasn't obvious. Still, two freak explosions in one night?

He summoned some of his men for a conference in the carpark. This is the conference that would later come to be referred to as 'the conference in the car-park,' although nothing of any importance would transpire during it. But Weber could not know that as the men gathered, and he wondered what he was going to tell them. 'We may be dealing here with –' What? A talking duck? A man from hell? '– an anomaly.' Great. He'd have to do better than that.

When the cop who was escorting him left the back seat of the patrol car to meet with his chief, Phil Blumburtt's first reaction had been to try to take a nap. He just wasn't any good if he didn't get his seven hours, and it was closing in on six in the morning of the most exhausting night of his life.

Second most exhausting night. Worse had been the time back in college. He'd stayed up all night with a stunningly beautiful sorority girl – mane of black hair, glittering blue eyes – he'd met at a mixer, debating the relative merits of evolution and creationism, and hoping that he'd score.

'But evolution's just another theory,' she'd said, her complexion as free of flaws as her head was of brains. 'Whereas the Lord is real.'

'How do you *know* the Lord is real,' he'd hammered away at her, a fiery undergraduate indignant on behalf of science. 'How do you *know* –'

'Because I believe in Him,' she explained.

'AHA! "Believe!" He had her now. 'It's your *opinion* –!'

'No,' she said, shaking her head. 'It's the truth. How could the world exist if someone didn't make it?' She laughed and tossed her dazzling hair. 'I mean, this all can't have come from nowhere!'

He wanted to grab her. He wanted to plunge his face into that hair. He wanted to say, 'Yes, yes, you're right. I'll agree with anything you say. The Lord. Satan. The Virgin Mary. Angels, devils, and little flying babies with harps. Anything. Just come back to my room.' Instead he said, 'It *developed*. It *evolved*.'

'From what?'

'Primal stuff!'

'Who made the primal stuff?'

'The Big Bang.' He paused to leer at her. She didn't get it, or pretended not to. 'I know, I know,' he went on. 'Your next question is, who made the Big Bang? My theory is, eternal cyclicity. Matter condenses, goes Big Bang, flies apart. Aeons pass. It loses momentum, and gets drawn back towards the centre, by gravity. Then there's another Big Bang. And so on. In. Out. In. Out.' He had to pause to control himself. She looked interested. He was compelled, as always, by the clarity of his own explanations. He had a talent for this. 'Meanwhile,' he concluded gently, inches from conquest, 'within those cycles, evolution determines the development of life-forms.'

'How do you know that?'

'Because of science.' He went on in a rush. 'Techniques can be verified. Results can be reproduced. Things can be measured objectively, at different places, in different times. Regardless of anyone's subjective feelings or beliefs.'

'What's wrong with private feelings and beliefs?'

'Nothing!' he hastened to soothe her. 'Private feelings are important. Very important. Feelings of warmth and friendship. Feelings of attraction and desire – they're all tremendously, tremendously significant –'

'So you believe in the Lord too, then.'

'No. I don't. Not really. I mean not at all. I believe in science.'

'But that's a belief too. You have faith in science, and I have faith in creationism.'

136

'But science is true, and creationism is a bunch of literal-minded mythology –'

'Maybe science is a bunch of mythology. How do you know it's true?'

'BECAUSE IT IS, YOU STUPID IDIOT!'

All that careful argument and dazzling logic wasted on a numbskull who actually believed that, six thousand years ago, God had made ten-million-year-old fossils for the purpose of fooling scientists. Phil had stomped around in a fury until sunrise, then had to go to classes.

Still, exhausted more than at any other point in his life but one, Phil couldn't relax. Because there was another cop in the driver's seat up front. Not to mention the fact that Phil was in handcuffs. He was under arrest! He was *in custody*! He would have a record! They'd haul him 'down-town' and throw him in a holding cell like some sleazebag on *Hill Street Blues*! He stared out of the window of the cop car at some dumb wishing well for tourists, complete with crank-handle and bucket on a rope.

And duck.

He looked again. Two eyes had risen up slowly from the well and had started in recognition when they'd met his. Phil held his breath and tried not to draw any attention to the fact that Howard the Duck was climbing out of the well and scurrying over to the car. Phil carefully, with both cuffed hands, rolled down his window.

'Howard!' he whispered. 'They arrested me at the plant! I'm gonna do hard time in the Big House!'

'Hard time?' Howard snorted. 'You hairless apes won't have any time to go to anybody's house if we don't stop Jenning.'

'It's convict slang,' Phil began to explain. 'Hard time means – huh? Jenning? What happened?'

'He's kidnapped Beverly!' Howard looked around, then slowly and very quietly opened the car door. 'Let's go!'

Phil Blumburtt faced a moment of decision. He could

remain in the car and face charges, a trial, utter humiliation. Or he could escape! And ally himself with the first extra-terrestrial duck ever to visit earth! And secure exclusive rights to a story that almost certainly would put him on the best seller lists, the lecture circuit, and the talk shows, from *A.M. Good Morning, Cleveland*! to Carson, Letterman, Ted Koppel and probably (why not?) PBS itself!

Some decision.

They tiptoed away from the car, and had little difficulty losing themselves in the activity around the fallen café. Phil grabbed a trash barrel and Howard jumped in. Then the scientist rolled it towards the rear of the building in a brusque, bored blue-collar manner. Inside, Howard tumbled like clothes in a dryer. It was the opposite of fun. When Phil finally stopped in the shadow of a storage building, he tipped the barrel upright. Howard climbed deftly out and, with balletic grace, fell immediately on his face.

Howard sat up. 'Jenning went back to the plant with Beverly.'

'What?' Blumburtt managed to be exhausted and frantic at the same time. 'Why?'

'He's gonna bring down more of these monsters!'

'What monsters?'

Howard sighed, and felt around his jacket for a smoke. He'd give anything for a cigar. Never mind his beloved Quackanudos – at that point he'd have settled for an El Produckto. But he had nothing. 'You don't happen to smoke cigars, do ya, Philsy?' he asked.

'Howard, what monsters?'

Howard explained: about Jenning, about the Whatsis of Sominex, or whatever it was called, about the demons from the Nether Zone, everything. Blumburtt listened intently, reacting only with a series of rapid nods and a nonstop, droning, 'Uh-huh . . . uh-huh . . .'

Finally Blumburtt said, thoughtfully stroking his jawline, 'So Dr Jenning's mind and body are possessed by an incorporeal creature of pure energy dedicated to total evil and mass destruction.' He nodded. 'That might explain his odd behaviour.'

Howard snorted. 'He's got more on his mind than odd behaviour. He's got big plans. He's gonna invite a bunch of other monsters here and they're gonna party all over the planet! They're gonna destroy all human life and take over the Earth!'

'But, Howard!' Blumburtt gasped. 'This is awful! What about my career?'

'What about my getting home, ya jerk! And what about Beverly?'

'Yes, of course. What about Beverly. I was just going to say that.'

'We gotta get out of here!' Howard snorted. 'Come on, Philsy – use your brain!'

'Of course!' Blumburtt glanced wildly around. 'My brain . . .' He saw something interesting across the car-park. Then, something else happened. He had an idea in his brain. 'I think I'm going to regret this,' he said. 'But come on!'

They dashed out from the cover of the building, leapfrogging from the shelter of one parked car to another, until they came to a long trailer. Inside stood an odd shape, covered in a tarpaulin. 'Gimme a hand,' Blumburtt said. Still handcuffed, he managed, with Howard's help, to remove the tarpaulin. What stood revealed was a small, ultralight aeroplane.

'I knew it!' Phil said. 'I knew this was a plane.'

'A plane . . .?' Howard said. He looked worried. 'But . . . what's it doing here? In the middle of a parking lot for some roadside café?'

'I don't know,' Phil said. And with a touch of reverence in his voice that even he, stalwart empiricist that he was, might have conceded was not without its religious dimension, he said, 'I guess we're just very very very very very very very very very very very very very very lucky.'

'You think so, huh?' Howard regarded the aircraft with ill-disguised nervousness.

Blumburtt was leaning in the cockpit, examining the controls. 'Don't you?'

'Oh, Philsy . . . on my planet we have a saying about airplanes.'

'Really, Howard? What is it?'

'If God had meant ducks to fly, he wouldn't have taken away our wings.'

Phil gave a brief, polite, otherwise-engaged laugh, but Howard wasn't kidding. The ability of a massive hunk of metal to lift up into the air and proceed for hundreds or thousands of miles, had always seemed to Howard a sort of cheating. Something basic in the scheme of things was violated every time a plane took off or landed safely. Somehow, somewhere, nature must be toting up all these violations (Howard didn't even want to think about electricity; duck-kind was really looking for trouble with that) and one day would exact her revenge. It made Howard nervous.

Not that he had never flown. But commercial jets were so gigantic and heavy, you lost all sensation of flight and that made it bearable. One moment you were in a oddly designed bus, zooming along the ground. Then, for a few hideous moments, you felt the lift off and saw the very planet recede. That was the worst part (not counting landing) and the part that always sent Howard burrowing into whatever business-duck-pandering in-flight magazine was at hand. Once the craft had levelled off and begun cruising, Howard was fine. As long as it felt like standing still, he loved to fly.

Phil murmured something to indicate that, although he had been listening, he wasn't really paying attention. Howard stared at the delicate-looking machine. It did not promise the sensation of standing still while in flight. In fact it looked, while sitting stationary on the ground, as though it already was moving. The duck reflected bitterly on the astronomical odds against it, or anything like it, appearing in the car-park of Joe Roma's Cajun Sushi and noticed that the sky was lightening. Dawn was mere minutes away. And Blumburtt was nodding to himself about the instruments and the controls.

Howard, English major though he had been, was able to put two and two together. He gulped.

Thirteen

Somehow, despite everything going on around her – Dark Overlord at the wheel, destruction of humanity a real possibility, extraterrestrial duck presumably squashed flat on roadhouse car-park – Beverly had managed to fall asleep. It would be too much to claim that she slept 'like a baby'. No, she slept like a woman in a diesel cab beside a monster from outer space, hurtling through the Ohio countryside, exhausted. She awoke like one, too – jerked out of slumber by a screech of air brakes and an abrupt slowing of the cab.

Jenning, or whatever it was, had mercifully retracted his tongue. He was no longer using it to suck power out of the cigarette lighter. She was grateful. Except for a faint luminescent glow that surrounded him, and the tendency of his fingers to broadcast showers of orange sparks, he looked perfectly normal. He forced the cab into reverse and backed up furiously until a sign they had passed came into view.

CUYAHOGA NUCLEAR POWER PLANT.

'Power!' growled Jenning.

Bev could only whimper, 'Oh, no . . .' and hope that, if he brought her within range of another human being, she could find help.

The hope was short-lived, if you call this living. As soon as Jenning saw the security gate at the entrance to the plant, he made a U-turn and set off in search of a side road. He found one half a mile away, easily smashed through its token, unguarded chain link barricade, and drove up a hill. On the other side was the plant. When they reached the crest Beverly could see a security patrol car within its grounds, cruising on routine rounds and unaware of their existence.

'Good,' Jenning intoned.

He was starting to remind her of Animal, the Muppet maniac chained to his drum set, who spoke in monosyllables and ate whatever came within range. But this was no children's puppet show. This was – at least, it seemed (to the extent that she could still tell what was real) real – real.

How real was it? It was so real, Jenning revved the engine – a powerful one, capable of hauling a fully loaded trailer – and charged. They bounded down the hill and straight at the perimeter fence of the plant. They smashed through and came to a halt. Beverly waited for the alarms to sound.

Nothing. No sirens, no bells, no guys with drawn guns. The security at this place was, like, unreal. They could have been two terrorists seeking weapons-grade plutonium. Bev sank back in the seat, nearly physically ill with anxiety. If Jenning was not thwarted – if he actually was able to summon the other Dark Overlords and conquer the Earth – somebody at this plant was going to be in big trouble.

Inside, Public Relations Consultant Jeff Grossbach was doing what he did best: slinging baloney like some kind of Olympic champion.

He'd been excited to get the assignment of squiring the Congressional tour group around Cuyahoga. Flew in from New York, set up base camp at the Cleveland Hilton, no problem. Nuclear power had been on the ropes lately and when the firm was hired to upgrade its image Jeff had welcomed the challenge. He was the kind of guy you'd expect to see profiled in the Esquire Register of Leaders Under Forty. In fact he expected to be asked to appear in it any day now, which is why he kept the latest edition under his pillow. He changed it every November, when the new one came out.

It was only a matter of time. Jeff knew he was good – damn good. A winner-type. Good looking. In shape. Ran a lot, ate fish, placed a high value on 'being creative'. Was more afraid of failure than of death – which was impressive, because, unlike a lot of those non-death-fearing guys, Jeff hadn't had a personal experience with a deity. ('Yet,' he thought optimistically.) Maybe he was the kind of a guy who was kind of a workaholic, but hey, sue him, he liked his job.

'Oh, Jeff?' One of the two official plant guides sidled over to him and asked, 'Don't you think it might be a good idea to let them ask questions –?'

Jeff laughed. 'Forget it. They're here to be told what they already want to hear. That's what P.R. is all about. Questions just confuse everybody.'

'But –'

'Hey. I said no problem. Now trust me and let me do my job.'

Jeff slapped the idiot on the back and motioned for the tour to follow. He was playing these Congressmen like a violin. Impressing them with some facts and figures here. Scaring them with some projections of future electrical demand there. Jeff's only complaint was these two company tour guides the plant forced him to bring along. Strictly from Geek City, this pair – Midwestern hicks whose idea of professionalism meant wearing an Arrow shirt. But Jeff and the Congressmen had rapport, chemistry, the intangible *je ne comprends pas* that meant everything.

'I'll be honest with you, gentlemen,' he now said, leading the party across the main floor amid the giant humming machinery. 'This Three Mile Island, China Syndrome meltdown stuff – it's all history. The only meltdowns around here are the cheese sandwiches in the toaster-oven!'

The two tour guides laughed at this, but it was lost on the Congressmen. They just looked around nervously. Jeff tried follow-upping.

'Of course, you get near one of those sandwiches, it's ninety per cent fatal!' The gentlemen from our nation's capital did not find this risible. Pompous bureaucrats. Jeff led them on.

The two local guides waited until the tour group had passed before cutting off their forced, fake laughs. The one who had questioned Jeff then took the opportunity to refer to Jeff Grossbach as a 'New York jerkoff'. The other guide agreed, then indicated a man bringing up the rear of the tour.

'Look at him,' the guide said in hushed, amazed tones. 'These Washington guys take a real beating on these junkets.'

The man in question was sweaty, pallid, and needed a shave. His clothes were torn and looked partially burnt. His eyes were dark and crazed; the hair frizzed up from his head as though a current of electricity were constantly running through him. Had the two guides been able to see his hands clearly, they might have witnessed random sparks flickering about his fingertips. Had they been able to open him up like a jar and peer inside, they would have beheld one of the Dark Overlords from the Nexus of Sominus.

'Yeah,' the other guide said, shrugging to convey his expertise. 'Well, you know – sightseeing all day, booze and broads all night . . .'

The shuffling group of Congressmen had halted at a viewing window. On the other side was a giant reactor, duly marked with purple and yellow caution signs.

'This is the heart of the system,' Jeff Grossbach said. 'This baby pumps out three hundred thousand kilowatts of juice!' He noticed the wild-eyed guy in the rear of the group, staring ravenously at the reactor. Jeff smiled. He understood how this guy felt. Why? Because, like these career politicos, Jeff Grossbach understood *power*. 'Sound good, Congressman?'

'Delicious.'

This brought baffled glances from others in the group and a knowing chuckle from Jeff Grossbach. 'Delicious. I love it. This way, gentlemen.' He led them down the hall. The man who had just spoken held back, waiting for the group to move on.

When the Congressmen and their guides had turned a corner, he stood before the viewing window of the reactor and glared at it with demonic intensity, his eyes widening.

145

There was an explosion. The windows shattered. Alarms immediately began to blare and whoop. The man entered the area of the reactor just as a metal security gate slammed down in front of him. His eyes flared and the fence exploded into bits. He advanced to the steel door, the entrance to the reactor core itself and, with a particularly malevolent glare, blasted it open.

By then guards and security people had arrived. They saw the figure of Jenning standing before the roaring inferno and contemplating it as a swimmer might regard a particularly inviting lake. They drew guns and fired. Nothing had any effect. How could it? Bullets melted within inches of Jenning's body.

Meanwhile, several rooms away, Jeff Grossbach and his charges heard the gunshots.

'Is that small weapons fire?' a Congressman asked nervously.

'Sounds like some action,' Jeff said. 'Gotta check this out –'

'We're coming too,' one of the guides said.

'Hey, 'fraid not.' Jeff held out his hand. 'You stay here with the Congressmen.'

'Who do you think you are, Grossbach –' the other began.

'I'm the specialist hired to save your ass,' Jeff said – rather smartly, he thought. 'Now stay with these gentlemen and make sure they don't come wandering out. Someone could get hurt, and that's the last thing I need.'

The guides exchanged a look. Finally one said to the other, 'I'll call their limos.'

'Yeah, that's good,' Jeff Grossbach said, 'I want that transportation here fast and I mean yesterday.'

'Go to hell.'

Chuckling, Jeff Grossbach trotted out and down the hall towards the reactor. He knew it was smart of him to post the two company men there – let them take the heat until he found out what was going on. Plus it would be their ass in a sling if any Representative got rowdy. It was a sharp move but hardly surprising because, let's face it, Jeff knew how to delegate.

Jeff Grossbach turned a corner, banged through a door and pulled up dead. He stared in awe at the lone man before the reactor. It was the guy who'd said 'delicious'. Well, it wasn't Jeff's fault – who would have thought the guy was a terrorist? He felt his spirits sink.

It was damage control time. This incident would play havoc with Jeff's carefully choreographed safety campaign. Because there was absolutely no hope that bozo over there would live. Not after exposure to however many zillions of roentgens he was absorbing. They might be actually looking at the first fatality in American nuke history. Great. Jeff sought consolation in the hope that maybe this guy wasn't actually the first.

But say the guy was a terrorist and that he died. It was cold comfort. Whoever he was, they were witnessing a P.R. nightmare in the making. The plant's security setup would draw more scrutiny than Brooke Shields at the Cannes Film Festival. Congressional committees would wonder how the hell this guy got in. Had he been after plutonium or what? Had his bomb gone off prematurely? How much damage had this one jerk been able to cause? Was there an internal security problem? All good questions and all desperately calling for evasive action.

Not to mention the fact that the entire alphabet soup of terror/counterterror, espionage/counterespionage, national security/national insecurity organizations would get involved. Jeff knew someone who worked at Langley, who'd taught him a little song:

> Who're the leaders of the club
> And what's the game they play?
> M.I.6
> K.G.B.

U.S. C.I.A.
Pull the rug, install a thug
Then look the other way
M.I.6
K.G.B.
U.S. C.I.A.

Mickey Mouse (Donald Duck!)
Mickey Mouse (Donald Duck!)
Forever with the Cold War we'll get by . . .
(Bye! Bye! Bye!)

Bug the homes,
And tap the phones,
And go pick up your pay
M.I.6
K.G.B.
U.S. C.I.A.

Jeff Grossbach expected squads of those types tomorrow. And of course there'd be the inevitable N.R.C. hearing. The anti-nuke press would have a holiday. The whole cause of nuclear energy public relations would be set back twenty years. This would make Three Mile Island look like *My Fair Lady*.

Of course, the exposure – Jess Grossbach's exposure – would be phenomenal. After all, who would give the artfully worded press briefings? Who would deftly dodge the pertinent, impertinent questions? Who would read the highly informative never-apologize, never-explain summaries from the podium in the makeshift press office they'd set up with coffee and doughnuts? (And with quality stuff – Kona beans, ground fresh, and forget the supermarket vacuum can junk.) Who would garner admiring sidelong profiles in *The New York Times* ('Jeff Grossbach: Ferde Grofe Of Image

148

Orchestration') for his effective handling of what 'all concede is an impossible position'?

In other words, who would be able to use this whole extremely unfortunate incident as a springboard for the launching of his own public relations firm based in Washington and New York? And issue an eight-page bi-weekly P.R. newsletter for business and industry at two hundred dollars a pop? The Kid, is who. So maybe things weren't so bad . . .

Jeff Grossbach was still savouring that fantasy when the figure before the reactor began to move. A blinding white light enveloped him as he walked heavily into the nuclear maelstrom that lay beyond. Jeff Grossbach squinted. That reactor core, where there were no incandescent or fluorescent light sources save for a few bare-bulb work lights, was nonetheless *bright*.

He held up his hand to shield his eyes, and discovered, with the delight and wonder of a child, that he could see, within it, its skeletal structure. He admired his own bones for a few seconds, before the thought obtruded that he had absorbed almost as much radiation as the lunatic who'd caused all this.

Beverly was almost free. Jenning had tied her hands with cord and stowed her in the sleeping compartment of the cab, but he'd been in a hurry and the bonds weren't that tight. Or maybe he thought she was weak simply because she was a woman. Were aliens sexist? Probably.

Her wrists were raw, and felt like they were bleeding, but she was just about done. There. She got up, with difficulty, and tried the door. It opened! She burst out into the cab –

– where Jenning's face – distorted, glowing, monstrous, fiendish, hideous – glared at her from the driver's seat! He burned with energy, a livid mask of irradiated flesh! His body flickered in polarized and solarized and psychedelicized brilliance! He emitted a loathsome growl. Smoke issued from his very nose! Not for the first time, Beverly screamed. She screamed again. This was by far the worst date of her life.

Fourteen

The sun, rising mercilessly on the extraterrestrial horrors besetting Beverly Switzler, was at the very same time pouring noontime tanning rays on bathers along the Italian Riviera. It was also, simultaneously, sinking slowly in the West over China, where soon more than a billion people would go to sleep. All this, accomplished by the same sun. You could board a sleek Concorde, jet briskly across the Atlantic while admiring the in-cabin 'MACH' groundspeed display and flying too fast for the screening of an in-flight movie, land in London, look up and see the same sun you left behind in New York. Think about it.

Or don't think about it. If not thinking about it, think about this: that that selfsame sun was at that very moment sheding sore-needed illumination on Howard the Duck and Phil Blumburtt. Same sun. As with the Riviera beach tanners, Chinese sleep-goers, and Beverly Switzler tongue-starer. The identical physical object. Put it this way: if, somehow, you were able to move close enough to the sun to apply a felt-tip pen to its surface and write, QUIT YOUR JOB FOR 'BOB', some individual in, say, New Zealand or someplace, would be able to look up and see what you'd written. A total stranger. The same message. If he looked up while you were writing it, he would see you yourself, except, of course, he would see you as you had been eight minutes previously, since it takes that long for light from the sun to etc. It's something most of us don't spend much time thinking about, thank God.

Thus it was that this world-class, world-famous sun was able to rise and bathe Beverly and Howard alike in its solar rays. All this effulgent radiance caused Howard the Duck to wake up. He had been snoozing uneasily in the cockpit of the ultralight aircraft ever since he and Phil had discovered it. They had agreed to take a brief nap, until daylight, before attempting to execute Phil's arguably boneheaded plan.

Now Howard sat in the cockpit of the plane, alternately trying to shrug off sleep and dive deeper into it. It seemed a million years ago that he had trudged home from the office, cracked a cold one and settled down to another dull, vaguely depressing evening at home. Now here he was – wherever this was – on the run, aiding and abetting, chasing a monster and hoping for a miracle.

Wasn't this what he secretly wanted? Excitement, danger, unpredictability? Didn't he feel more alive than at any other time in his existence? Didn't this flirtation with disaster lend pungency to his every waking moment, help him to fully appreciate 'life' as he had never appreciated it before? Wasn't he exhilarated by the prospect of running from the Law? Didn't he, in fact, feel like a big shot, a tough bird, a duck-of-action? Weren't the risks he was running like a drug, jazzing up his system, getting the adrenalin flowing? Wasn't this the greatest time of his life? And, if not, wasn't it supposed to be? What was wrong with him, anyway? Just what was the problem with How Weird the Duck?

'Wait a minute,' he thought. He shifted in his seat and banged his knees on the wheel. 'Where am I getting all these thoughts? Where'd this junk in my mind come from? Who's doing the thinking here – me, or some stuff I read or heard twenty years ago?'

COVERAGE-IN-DEPTH INSERT 5
Pop Psychological Profile of Howard the Duck

Howard the Duck grew up in a suburban community typical of those that flourished, on Duck World, in the United Drakes, in the decades following Duck World War II. His parents, Samuel and Sylvia the Duck, were middle-class birds of unsophisticated, petty-bourgeois backgrounds. Sam worked in the power tool industry, as a middle-management executive with Quack and Ducker. Sylvia was a fulltime housewife.

Neither had attended college. Both, in some vague, never-discussed way, regarded their first-laid, Howard, as the means by which their family might, somehow, 'improve' its social status. The Ducks were eager to escape the oppressive pecking order and backbiting, flock mentality of their own inner-city ducklinghoods. And their rising economic prospects suggested that, indeed, they were 'moving up' in the world.

Accordingly, they dutifully imitated what they took to be a more refined code of manners. And they were scrupulous about teaching it to their son. Sam and Sylvia had grown up believing that, as regards the ruthlessness of social reality, 'it's a low-lying marshy swamp-like tidal basin out there.' Safe and sound in the suburbs, they now insisted their son grew up to be 'fair', 'good', 'considerate', and, most of all, 'a nice bird'.

A moody, intense young duck, Howard possessed a mind which dwelt naturally, not in realms of pictures or sounds or numbers, but in verbal abstraction. He gravitated towards the lofty, the philosophical. Add to this the fact that his exposure to art and literature was limited to the popular and the middlebrow, and it became inevitable that the first novel which made any significant impact on the bird was the then-popular answer to brooding individualism, *The Fountainhen*.

A brief summary of the novel suggests the hold it may have had on the duckling. Howard Stoark, a fiercely independent designer of chicken coops, resists every effort on the part of the rich and powerful to denature his vision and commercialize his designs. He is surrounded by cowards and fools, panderers to the masses, whose bad taste and meretricious ideas result in structures cobbled together out of a hodgepodge of classical and modern elements. Indeed, Stoark's 'arch-rival' – a spineless, contemptible impotent – wins fame and fortune with a design of a multi-storey coop resembling a grandfather clock, with immense round portholes on its sides and topped by a Chippendale-style broken pediment!

Stoark refuses to compromise, and in so doing alienates those around him. He encounters rejection, poverty and humiliation. But, thanks to his unswerving integrity and so forth, he wins the love of the only other character worthy of his respect. She is the most beautiful, wilful, tempestuous, brilliant, creative, fabulous duck in the world. Plus her father's rich. With her by his side, the novel climaxes with the creation of Stoark's masterpiece: a titanic, eighty-six-storey fountain in the shape of a chicken. Of course by then everybody says he's a genius.

It was from this crude, albeit evocatively written, novel that Howard the Duck first attained what we might call his philosophical self-awareness. He knew that he identified with Howard Stoark. For one thing, their first names were the same. But there were other similarities, which Howard (the Duck) carefully listed on a sheet of paper he hid from the rest of the world and his parents, in his dresser. Entitled 'Similarities with H.S,' it revealed that Howard (the Duck) had always conceived of himself as unique, highly individualistic, smarter than most and forever obliged to resist the mediocrity of those around him. *The Fountainhen*, a book that seemed written by a moody fourteen-year-old, made moody, fourteen-year-old Howard the Duck drunk on the possibilities of adolescent egotism.

Then Howard read *The Hatcher in the Rye*.

It awoke the other part of his soul, the selfless, sweet, innocent duckling who wanted nothing more than for everyone he knew to be happy. The story concerns a young duck who runs away from an orphanage (where parentless eggs are hatched), only to suffer a loss of his innocence when, in the city, he tastes his first shot of whisky – the 'rye' of the title. The book stirred the idealist in Howard. It inspired in him the contradictory emotions of altruism for humanity and contempt for society. It also inspired in him the desire to drink whisky – a negative effect, which presumably set the pattern for his rampant drug abuse in his college years, which was so irresponsible as well as illegal.

Several months later Howard – and the world – were enthralled by the film *Ducktor No* and by the depiction of its fictional super-spy hero, James Pond. Pond's self-sufficiency, his wry imperturbability, his unflappable success with female ducks and his consummate grace were all deeply compelling to the insecure, graceless, sexually intimidated adolescent duck. Also this (and all subsequent Pond movies) served to reinforce in Howard the assumption that private action could be effective. In Howard's idealistic duck's breast, that feeling was transposed into its philosophical counterpart, namely, that private *beliefs* were significant; that it *mattered* what stand he took and what opinions he held.

A cynical person can only regard this attitude with the cruellest of amusement.

Nonetheless, this view was to have a profound effect, both on Howard and on much of his generation, beginning at around the time of the release of the fifth Pond movie, *Thunderbill*. By then, the involvement of the United Drakes in a foreign war, without clear strategic mandate or popular validation, caused a great rift to develop between the adult society of the U.D. and its children. These were the same birds taught from the nest to be 'fair' and 'good' – to be, in a word, idealistic. Now they faced conscription to fight – and, possibly, die – in a war without adequate moral basis, and for a government uncertain of its own goals and inconsistent in its own ethical behaviour.

Inevitably, they rebelled. Howard the Duck, exulting in the freedom of college, joined his peers in condemning

United Drakes society. He spent his college years ignoring study ('The university is inherently gullshit,' a campus radical explained to him one afternoon, at a 'workshop' on 'Corporate Profits and the War.') Howard, like so many of the most interesting, compelling, or creative students he knew, spent his undergraduate years 'experimenting' with drugs, listening to and playing politically defiant rock 'n' roll music and consolidating in himself the belief that having fun was a political act.

His reading and viewing reinforced this attitude. *Hatch-22*, *Bird of the Rings*, *That Was The Beak That Was*, *One Flew Over the Cuckoo's Nest* – all denounced the established order, or featured heroic efforts to defy and defeat institutionalized evil.

Then the war ended. The draft was abolished. The generation that had booed the villain off the stage now discovered that, without him, the play was boring. One day Howard succumbed to the inevitable. He graduated and went out into the world.

He found it a place where enormous energy and attention was given over to trifles long-dismissed and lies long-discredited. The cause by which he had discovered his social identity was, overnight, obsolete. He was left with his individualist's feelings of importance without a meaningful social context in which to exercise them – Howard Stoark without his chicken coops. All anyone talked about now was 'lifestyle'. That seemed little more to him than an obsession with things to buy. Howard had seen through that years before, which dovetailed neatly with the fact that he had no money.

He tried this job and that, went from poetry to med. school, but nothing had any meaning. Indeed, 'having meaning' had no meaning; it was simply a cliché from the postwar 'self-improvement' fad. As he got older, and people he knew began to be 'successful', he started to feel insecure, so he took a job at the ad agency. At least (and at last) he began making money. Meanwhile, he still harboured his feelings of idealism, his suspicion of social institutions, his identity as an outsider.

The old rebel impulses remained. But the world now belonged to those who could serve the corporation – many of whom had been Howard's protesting classmates. It blew his birdbrain to see how blithely they now dismissed that era, how casually they now betrayed everything they had supposedly once stood for. Among them, Howard felt like a duck who's arrived at a party in costume, only to find everyone else in formal wear. His idealism curdled into cynicism. He became a grump, a grouch, a crab.

And the main target of his crabbiness became himself. He had contempt for the very beliefs he was still proud to hold. He called himself a chump for not being more like the very ducks he despised. In short, he became a self-loving, self-hating, future-fearing neurotic, obsessed with money, insecure about success, and resolving daily to 'get his quack together' and realize his 'dream'. Like so many of his fellow Americanards, he was half-hypnotized into trying to jazz up the present by injecting into it a fantasy about the future. The result: every day he felt a little more diminished, a bit more insulted, a touch more behind schedule. He was the perfect citizen of the United Drakes in the year 1986 A.D. (Accurate Ducktime).

Thus it was that, on awakening in the cockpit, Howard the Duck challenged himself for not being delighted with his new role as outlaw/castaway/fugitive. Wasn't that how he had fancied himself back in college?

'Yeah, I guess so,' he thought, climbing out. 'Or maybe I just pretended to. That was during a wild time. It all seems so long ago now.' He was starting to remind himself of a few of his father's friends, veterans of Duck World War II. The most exciting moments of their lives had come in the War, when they were nineteen. They had settled for tedium, routine, and nostalgia for the next five decades. Or so it seemed. 'Anyway, I could sure use a shower and a cuppa.'

'You're up. Good.' Phil Blumburtt had roused himself and was instantly in high gear. 'Let's unload the aircraft and put her through pre-flight.'

In the cockpit of the ultralight plane they'd found crash helmets and goggles. It was like finding the keys waiting in a Jaguar parked on the street. In fact, they found the ignition keys to the plane, too. But that sort of thing happened every day on television, and what was the life of Howard the Duck, if not television by other means? So they suited up.

'Look, Philsy,' Howard said nervously, as they wheeled the plane off its trailer and deployed its wings. 'You sure you know how to work this?'

'Sure,' Blumburtt said, frowning at the cockpit. 'Theoretically, anyway . . .'

'This isn't a theoretical plane,' Howard said. 'It's real.'

Phil motioned for Howard to climb in the front seat. He got behind him. 'If you were a scientist, Howard,' he said, settling in, 'you'd know that theory is real, too.'

'If you were a duck,' Howard said, 'you'd know the difference between real flying and theoretical flying.' He sighed. 'Anyway, let's go. I just hope you know what you're doing.'

'Don't worry. I'll start her up, and you take over.' Blumburtt yanked on the D-handle of the starter cord. The engine spluttered, then died.

'ME?'

'Howard. I've still got the cuffs on. Get ready.' He yanked again.

It caught. The engine wasn't much bigger than one you'd find on a decent power mower, and the cargo of two bodies strained the craft to its limit . . . but the ultralight began to taxi across the car-park.

'Howard!' Phil yelled. 'Grab the joystick!'

'What's that?'

158

'Give it more throttle! More throttle!'

'More what?'

The plane was like a hang-glider with a motor. As it rolled along the car-park Howard got the full impact of every minute bounce and jiggle. He worked pedals and pulled sticks. Panels on the wings waved up and down; rudderlike wafers on the tail assembly waggled. Fifty yards away, Howard could see Lieutenant Weber in tired conference with his men. Blowing this would put both of them in the slammer. Howard shut his eyes and pulled the joystick.

'Good!' Phil yelled. 'More!'

They were airborne! They had actually lifted off the ground! Four feet, at least! Howard felt triumph surge through every fibre of his being and glanced wildly around until – 'YAAAAH!' – they fell and bounced and rolled, groundborne once again.

'More pedals! More stick!' Phil hollered.

Howard could see the cops scatter to their cars. The vehicles revved up, roof lights came on and started spinning, sirens whooped to life, and the cops squealed across the car-park in pursuit. This was it. If they were going to cheat Nature and actually fly they'd better do it now. Howard gave the joystick a definitive pull.

'Great! Now steady the pedals!' Blumburtt shouted.

They were up. It was amazing. And no mere four measly feet, either. They must have been, oh, at least ten feet in the air.

'I don't like this!' Howard screamed. 'I don't like this at all!'

The cop cars lurched out of the car-park and onto the highway, following the plane's course. Joe Roma's was on the outskirts of a suburban development and it was through this placid, manicured community Howard now piloted (or was piloted by) the plane. Milkmen, mailmen, other men and women suburbanites of every stripe stopped and gawked and summoned their various kids and honeys to watch, as the duck-piloted craft flew smack down the centre of the street, not much higher than the basketball rims on garage backboards. Those keen of ear may have heard the plane's pilot and co-pilot conversing, thus:

'We're too low!' Howard squawked over the motor's drone.

'Too much weight!' Phil nodded, his eyeball calculations having proven correct. 'It'll take some time to get altitude –'

'We don't have some time! Look!'

They were heading directly for a mail truck. Collision could mean catastrophe – the very efficiency of the United States Postal Service hung in the balance. 'The right pedal!' Phil shouted. 'The right pedal!'

Some ducks have the right stuff. All Howard had was the right pedal. He leaned on it just as the mailman bailed out and hit the pavement. The plane lifted the crucial two inches and banked right. The community breathed a grateful prayer of thanks. The mail would go through – through some guy's living room, actually, as the driverless mail truck ploughed up a kerb and across a lawn, smack into a bay window.

Meanwhile the cop cars screamed by in pursuit.

Howard opened his eyes. They were over the outskirts of town. Beneath them, a loudspeaker on the roof of one of the police cars was blaring 'LAND THE AIRCRAFT! LAND THE AIRCRAFT IMMEDIATELY!'

It was mesmerizing to observe how the car beneath kept perfect pace with them. Howard had that agreeable sensation of stasis-in-motion you sometimes get when a train parallelling your train runs beside it in the same direction, at the same speed. Movement feels momentarily cancelled. For one giddy instant, you seem stationary, while the world out of the other window appears to be in motion. Einstein knew all about this sort of thing.

Perhaps Einstein should have been flying the plane. He might have noticed, before Howard did, that they were heading directly for a freeway overpass. When Howard finally did spy the looming bridge, he did the only sensible thing. He began to talk to the aeroplane.

'Up, plane, up!' he cried.

'We'll never make it over!' Blumburtt screamed.

'Down, plane, down!'

The ultralight swooped, down not up, and zoomed under the bridge – it passed under the overpass – just as three police cars screamed in from the opposite direction. They swerved, scattered, fishtailed and spun out like stunt drivers in a car chase. The plane left them behind and made for open country.

Phil leaned forward and pointed. 'We can lose them if we get away from the road!'

Howard nodded. It was a good idea. Too often, in movies and on TV, he'd watched chase scenes where a car, for example, bore down on a duck on foot. And the duck on foot would try – always in vain – to outrun the car. Not once did the duck on foot ever think to *get off the road*. Not once did the pedestrian bother to run in any but a straight line, on the highway, giving his pursuer precisely the advantage he needed. It was refreshing, then, to hear Phil suggest this sensible tactic.

'Good man, Philsy!' Howard turned the joystick, sending the craft out across an open field.

Unfortunately, the cops were not deterred. They too veered off the road and bounced across the field. Still, a plane versus a few cars – how could it be any contest?

The ultralight zoomed across a farm: picturesque furrows, rocket-like silo, munching cows, futilely barking god named King, the whole catastrophe. The farmer, jouncing merrily atop his tractor, saw the plane heading for him and jumped off at the last instant. The tractor continued, driverless, as the plane kept on keeping on. They flew through a farmyard; farm animals, assembled in archetypal array as though summoned from Central Casting, scattered on cue. They flew close to a small pond; birds rose up from its shimmering

161

surface, squawking and flapping like the actual, palpable ducks they so humorously were.

'Sorry, guys,' Howard muttered.

They were still over fields, and the cop cars were still bounding after them. To the side they spied a dirt road – and two more cop cars could now be seen streaking down its dusty length, parallel to their flight, brown clouds of topsoil billowing out behind them. It was about time for a new development . . .

It came in the form of gunfire. Policemen were leaning out of the windows and shooting.

'I forgot!' Phil said. 'It's open season.'

'Not funny! Not funny!'

If 'bullets whistled past, narrowly missing their mark,' Howard couldn't hear 'em. His attention was captured by the next obstacle in their steeplechase. It was a windbreak, a row of trees specifically chosen to be tall. The row was too long to go around.

'LOOK OUT!' Phil suggested. 'PULL UP!'

Howard yanked the joystick like a slot machine addict on a hot streak. The plane lifted. And lifted. And lifted! They were up – and over the treetops, just brushing the highest leaves. Howard could feel the scratch of twigs on the under-belly of the fuselage through the thin metal skin. There was a rasp, a sound of clattering and rubbing, and then a sudden sense of release. They were past.

Behind them, the cops skidded to a halt, stymied by an irrigation ditch that blocked their way. Their sirens died and their guns stopped shooting. For one breathless instant there was, more or less, peace. Ahead of pilot and co-pilot lay the city. They flew on.

Fifteen

Beverly and her atomic-powered escort roared down the highway in the truck cab. Actually, she had to admit, Jenning was taking fairly good care of her, considering that he was essentially a monster from hell. She knew that he had his reasons, that he intended to use her body as a host-vessel for receiving and harbouring another demon of inconceivable evil and so forth. But as long as the two of them didn't reach the Aerodyne labs, she was okay. True, this was the attitude of the man who, having fallen off the Empire State Building, told a concerned observer on the forty-fifth floor, 'So far, so good.' But the alternative was fear – stark, unreasoning terror. And she was too tired for that.

They reached a line of cars, bumper to bumper, and a sign that blinked 'Slow For Smog Inspection.' That was illogical, on this major highway, and unlikely, considering that smog inspections were usually conducted at gas stations and repair shops under state supervision. But there it was. Jenning growled and reluctantly slowed down.

Up front, a line of state troopers spoke to the drivers as they pulled up and stopped. One such trooper stopped one such driver and said, 'Smog inspection. I'd like to know the age of this vehicle and see your registr –'

The car into which the cop was leaning crept forward. It had the effect of dragging the trooper a foot or so down the road.

'I said stop the vehicle,' the trooper said. 'Engine off. Please. Let me see your regis –'

The car jumped an additional few feet. It cranked the trooper's annoyance up an additional notch or so. 'I said engine off!' he barked.

'It is off!' the driver snapped. When something wasn't his fault, he could be as fearless with authority figures as the next guy. 'Somebody behind's pushing!' This whole smog thing was a big pain in the butt, but it sure felt good to yell back at a cop. He jerked his thumb to the rear. 'Talk to *him*!'

The cop straightened and peered up the line. The source of the disturbance, obviously, was the monster diesel cab, its vertical exhaust stack smoking, the wiseguy at the wheel leaning forward as though ready to plough through the whole crowd. As the trooper watched, the cab reared back and ground forward into the next car, prodding the whole line ahead two feet. Very funny. The trooper walked towards it with elaborate care.

In the cab, Beverly gulped. Horns were honking, state cops closing in. Maybe she should try to make a break –

'WHAT THE HELL IS THIS?' the cop snapped. 'Get out of that vehicle. Turn off that engine!'

Bev grabbed the door handle. Maybe while Jenning was distracted –

What happened next held even her attention.

Jenning raised his hand and with an airy gesture, a mere finger raised towards the cop, released a ray of . . . well, some sort of energy. It hit the trooper and set his body in uncontrollable motion. The other police, and motorists who had got out to watch, stared dumbly as the trooper vibrated, shuddered and seemed to dissolve into his component atomic parts. Imagine the image of your favourite fictional TV character – Blake or Alexis, Crockett or Tubbs, Johnny or Ed, Nancy or Ron – in that eyeblink of an instant just before it dissolves to commercial. The ungraspable evanescence, the utter discorporation, the sheer now-you-see-it-now-you-don't-ist disappearance. Got it? The guy went away.

It happened with a bang – a sudden violent explosion in which the strong force (which held the nucleus together) blew up a member of the police force (which held the civilization together). Which is to say that the trooper – or, rather, the sum of molecules which, when added together, equalled 'the trooper' – flew apart. Other cops pulled their weapons, yelled (pointlessly) 'Freeze!' and shot into the cab. The windshield shattered. Bullets ripped into upholstery. Beverly screamed, cringing and crying and petrified. Jenning roared. His eyes opened wide, and then flared –

The entire inspection station was engulfed in a god-forsaken atomic explosion. Bev had to shield her eyes from the magnesium-white radiance that arose as the cars, the people, the landscape, the innocently bystanding flora and fauna went up in a cataclysmic (and not-unorgasmic) release, as the matter of these various organic and inorganic bodies returned to its primal state of roiling energy. Bev's retinas, even protected by her hands, glowed red, as a deafening roar resounded throughout the landscape, and a rich, dense, dark mushroom cloud rose in sluggish archetypicality.

After the roar had subsided and the cloud dispersed, there came a stillness. Beverly removed her hands and opened her eyes. A profound nothing was in evidence. Some smoke, some small residual flames dying down, the odd bird limping by. But the total number of cars and people visible to the naked eye equalled zero. Jenning smiled.

'We passed the inspection.'

Great. Alien humour.

He floored the gas pedal and the cab roared through the smoking devastation. Bev decided that, unless help arrived fairly soon, she would probably throw in the towel and simply proceed to lose her mind.

Meanwhile, a couple of thousand feet above Cleveland . . .

Howard was getting the hang of it. The thrill of flying – it wasn't bad, actually. That big broad patchwork landscape spread beneath them, receding gently at the horizon as the Earth itself revealed its curve. The tiny cars tooling along narrow, ribbon-like roads. Sun glinting off windows and water. Clouds in amorphous formations, drifting towards them in group after group, one snowy range after another deliquescing to insubstantial murk as the plane moved through them.

Howard took a deep breath: it was brisk, cold, stunningly refreshing. In fact it left him a little lightheaded. After all the travail of the past twelve hours, that gulp of upper atmosphere had the mood-lifting impact of a nice snort of Johnny Squawker Black. I could get used to this, Howard thought. Maybe we could just go on forever, flyin' around in the old ultralight, me and old Philsy –

They'd fly from town to town, two guys and a plane. Okay – one guy, one bird, and a plane. They'd have adventures, wacky mis- or otherwise. They'd set down in some quiet American hamlet, draw suspicious stares from the locals, hire themselves out to earn spending money – Howard doing odd jobs, maybe writing some ad copy here and there, Phil finding work as a freelance palaeontologist.

They'd get involved with the unhappy wives of driven alcoholic businessmen, help a blind kid find the courage to take piano lessons, raise money for the local Gilbert and Sullivan group, teach a tough sheriff the true meaning of justice, bring together a husband and wife on the verge of a tragic breakup, reconcile two estranged brothers, make it easier for a lonely old millionaire to face death – stuff like that. They'd be the best of friends, get drunk together, save each other's lives, steal each other's shaving cologne and punch each other on the shoulder. God, it would be wonderful. Howard would stand up for Phil when some local bully bad-mouthed Charles Darwin. Phil would intervene when some tough guy made one anti-duck remark too many.

Then, somewhere near Louisville, Kentucky, they'd have a falling out, over – what else? A girl.

She'd be the daughter of the local rich man, and pure poison. Phil would go for her in a big way, but Howard could see she was trouble. He'd try to make his friend realize, but the guy would be gone, just gone. Phil would turn on

Howard, accuse him of being jealous. Him! Howard the Duck! Who only cared about his friend not getting his heart handed to him on a platter! Man, that would hurt. But Howard would take it. Why? Because the guy was his friend, that's why. Because that's what you do when a guy's your friend, period, is why.

Meanwhile, Phil would try to impress her and her snooty country club friends – the thin, sarcastic tennis champ; the chubby, drawling parlour wit; the short-haired, bitchy best girlfriend; the smug, uptight organizer-type. There Phil would be, showing off all his palaeontology at some catered picnic with caviar and runny cheese, talking about the universe and all. Those phoneys! They wouldn't be good enough to hold his lab coat! They'd pretend to find him 'fascinating', to want to hear all about the evolution of sense organs in the lower mammals. Yeah, sure. In a pig's eye! The whole time they'd be secretly laughing up their sleeves at him, mocking him behind his back. The way he talked fast about fossils, and came from Cleveland, and hung around with a three-foot duck who wrote ad copy.

Howard would have to trick the girl into revealing her true nature. How? He had it! He'd come on strong to her! Make like it was her he had eyes for, and the heck with his friendship with Phil. She'd dig it. Not only for his innate animal magnetism, but she'd love being the cause of this big betrayal. (Her type lived for that sort of thing.) Then, when Howard had her all primed for a big romantic assignation one night, he'd bring Phil along and somehow trick him into hiding in the bushes. Let him hear the girl telling Howard how she loved *him*, wanted to run away with *him*, wanted to die for *him*. Sure, it'd just be more of her typical baloney, but Phil wouldn't know that . . .

Problem is, she'd mean it! For the first time! She'd say, 'Howard, I . . . I never knew it could be like this.' He'd say, Aw nuts. 'It's true,' she'd say. 'I know I've been bad – to your friend Phil, and to oh, so many other men. But you've shown me something I suppose I never thought I could have . . .'

And, well – he'd be tempted! Who wouldn't? Because he could tell that, for once in her life, she was sincere. She really loved him. And there Phil would be in the bushes, hearing it all. What would Howard do?

He'd tell her to take a walk. He'd turn her down, and with his pal he'd make tracks. It wouldn't be easy – but it would be the right thing.

As for Phil – well, it would hurt the guy – at first. But strong sickness required strong medicine. And he'd get over it. Howard would see to that. They'd jump back in the ultralight and head off for somewhere, anywhere, whatever was over the next horizon. Anyplace they had beer on tap and fresh cigars in a box and a few laughs you could get your hands on. And one day Phil would thank Howard. Oh, not tomorrow, or the next day. But some day. Howard could wait. Still, Howard knew, something in Phil would die a little that night in the bushes. What a shame guys didn't automatically fall for gals (and drakes for ducks) that were good for them! What a damn shame . . .

'I'm sorry, Phil,' Howard said, swallowing the lump in his throat. 'But I had to do it. She was gonna break up the team! And she didn't really love you, man. I could tell, you gotta believe that –'

'Howard, you're babbling. Must be the thin air up here.' Blumburtt checked his seat belt. 'There's Aerodyne. Get ready to land.'

Howard shook his head. He must have dozed off at the wheel, or flipped out into some sort of oxygen-deprivation daydream. What was it? Something about meeting some snooty tennis player in the bushes? He'd be glad to get down, and out of this thing. He looked where Phil pointed, and saw the plant drawing nearer below. The truck-cab that had once nearly mown him down was parked in front.

Then he realized what his co-pilot had said. Howard grew panicky.

'What? Land? I don't know how to land!' The engine coughed and rasped. Blumburtt held up a transparent plastic hose just as a last little dribble of liquid gurgled through it.

'You're about to learn,' he said. 'We're out of gas . . .'

The ultralight nosed sharply earthward and fell, obedient to the law of gravity. Its two passengers fell with it, obedient to the fact they were strapped inside. Howard pulled on the joystick, but got nothing. 'This won't work!' he hollered. 'Think of something else! Fast!'

Blumburtt looked around the cockpit. A red emergency ring looked promising. He gave it a yank.

There was a small explosion. At first Howard thought it more ground fire from cops, assembled and waiting – who knew how? – at Aerodyne. Then he felt a jerk, banged his knees on the instrument panel and realized that a canopy had opened above them, slowing their fall and imparting to it a pleasant, Ferris-wheel-like rocking. And it wasn't just a parachute for him or Phil; no, this was attached to the plane itself. Just as he was beginning to enjoy this leisurely float to earth, they hit. There was a compressed crunch of plane, chute, duck, and palaeontologist. The two passengers scrambled out of the wreckage.

'Are you okay?' Phil asked. When Howard nodded Phil said, 'Good. Now, how the hell are we supposed to stop this guy?'

Howard looked at him, eye to eye. 'Beverly said there are no accidents in the universe. She said maybe I was sent here for some cosmic purpose . . .' He set off, determined and, now that the flight was over, completely fearless.

'So what?' Blumburtt ran to keep pace with the manfully striding duck. They headed in the direction of the rear of the Aerodyne building. 'I mean, hey. Don't get me wrong.

Beverly's a nice girl – woman, sorry – a nice woman. But just because she talks about a cosmic purpose doesn't mean it makes any sense.'

They took cover as police and workers appeared, going about their business. 'Look, Phil,' Howard said, dead serious. 'Isn't it a little too coincidental, that the laser spectroscope would bring me here before it brought the Dark Overalls from the Necklace of Sominex?'

'Not necessarily.'

'Couldn't it have been maybe directed by some Cosmic Protector . . . who hit his intended target . . . which was me . . .'

'Howard . . .' The scientist sighed. 'Hit you for what purpose?'

'So I'd be here . . .' Howard paused, then plunged on. 'To save Beverly . . . and this whole planet.'

'Um, Howard?' Phil sought a tactful way to describe to the duck that he, the duck, was insane. 'You shouldn't be in Cleveland. You should try California. There are people there who'll pay you big money to make a TV show out of that. There are others who will worship you as God. Either way, it's a living.'

Howard headed for the rear door to the plant. 'Let me put it in terms you'll understand, Phil. Maybe I was sent here to keep all you hairless apes from becoming extinct. Like your dinosaurs.'

'But that's nuts! Which doesn't bother me, particularly, because hey, I can be a nutty guy. But it's unscientific!'

'You got a better explanation?'

'Ah . . . no.'

'Phil,' Howard paused at the door. 'I've been complaining the whole time I've been here. Waiting for someone to help me. It's like, inside, part of me thought I didn't deserve any better. Well, I do. And now I'm gonna help myself. If I have to save the Earth to get home, then that's what I'll do. I'm ready to fight.'

Blumburtt nodded. Then, with difficulty, he said, 'I guess I haven't been much help, huh? I got all excited about what you were and how I could make the most of it –'

'Forget it,' the duck said briskly. 'I need your help now. I know I called you a jerk and an idiot and a fraud and a lamebrain and a numbskull and a nitwit and –'

'Uh, Howard –?'

'– face and a chowderhead and –'

'Howard?'

'– but I take it all back. You're smart and you've got guts.'

'Hey.' Blumburtt looked embarrassed. He chucked the duck under his chin. 'You're a beautiful guy.'

'I'm a duck, Phil.'

'Whatever.'

They went inside.

It was easy to dash down the main hall towards the central lab; a drastically reduced work contingent had left the place unusually empty. At the lab door Howard and Blumburrt paused, then darted in and hid near some big scientific-type equipment of some kind. Heavy breathing and light clicks and clacks came from further in the lab. They leaned out and looked.

It was Beverly, strapped to a metal table beneath the laser spectroscope, Frankenstein-style. Phil nudged the duck and pointed; to the side, the hulking form of Jenning could be seen hovering over the controls, flicking and adjusting and punching and comparing. His eyes were inexpressive, like a zombie's – but they radiated heat and a sicko sort of light. His body glowed.

'He's running the activation sequence!' Phil whispered.

'Jeez, he's going to bring down another Dark Overlord! We gotta get Bev outa here!' Howard started to make his presence known, to confront the awful fiend –!

Phil grabbed him and pulled him back. 'Hold it. What are you going to stop him with? Your good looks? We need something – I got it!' He dragged the duck back outside into the hall. 'Come on.' He started trotting; Howard had to waddle double-time to keep up. 'Carter once showed me something that could do the job. If we can find it . . .'

Sixteen

The Neutron Disintegrator: Weapon of the Unforeseeable Future

The Neutron Disintegrator (N.D.) was the President's idea.

It came to him during his customary Saturday morning cartoon viewing. In fact it was kind of a cute story, one which he would repeat endlessly for the rest of his life to the press, White House aides, the Cabinet, visiting diplomats, heads of state, his wife, total strangers and the Pope.

It seems he had just reached into the cereal box on his lap to pull out the last sticky fistful of Sugar Pops, when a particularly thrilling shoot-out on *Humongor: Power-Shah of Space and Time* (featuring Beau-Clara, It-girl of the Universe) propelled him into an almost uncontrollable fit of thinking. By the time the commercials began for the Humongor Action Toy, the Beau-Clara Action Wardrobe, the Humongor Power-Shah-Zammer Beam Gun Ensemble, the Beau-Clara Action Wig Collection, and the Humongoer Book Bag/Lunch Box Action School Supply Material Consignment Kit, the President was moved to verbalize his thoughts.

'You know,' he remarked to his Chief of Staff, who leaned over to hand his boss a napkin. 'What if we had one of those ray guns, to have, so you'd – there'd be a situation that a device, where you'd have a secure ability. For defensive, because missiles, and so forth.'

'I think that's an excellent idea, Mr President,' his Chief

of Staff replied. Gently, he replaced the empty box with a new one of Smurfberry Crunch.

'Me too!' added the Secretary of Defence. He pulled down the sleeves of his pyjamas and re-tied his bathrobe in a double knot. The darn thing often seemed to come loose of its own accord. It was annoying. He'd worked hard to ingratiate himself with the government's power establishment and fight Communism; the last thing he or the country needed was for his credibility to be impaired by having his bathrobe fall off during one of these cartoon breakfasts. 'We'll need a couple of billion for a feasibility study –'

'Well, now, hold on,' the president said, shaking his head and trying to suppress a twinkling smile. (He couldn't quite suppress it. He never could. He was a fundamentally happy man.) 'When you say "billion," is that the same as "million?" '

'Essentially, yes, Mr President.'

'I thought so, and so yes, go ahead with the study.'

The Pentagon formed a Special Advisory Board to investigate the feasibility of the project. The group was blue ribbon all the way. To assure their impartiality, they were hand-picked by the Secretary of Defence himself, with input from the Joint Chiefs. The team consisted of:

– scientists who made their livings and reputations working on defence research grants. These were the professionals. Because their very livelihoods depended on work they did for the Pentagon, they had to do a good job in deciding if all that money should be spent on this visionary weapon. Because if they didn't, then they – and the country – knew that the Pentagon would get mad. And then where would they be?

– military officials destined to work for weapons firms after retirement. How could these men, too, even show their faces at their future jobs, unless they had really tried hard to assess the value of this new system?

– defence industry executives. These were the no-nonsense guys who knew what it meant to produce sophisticated hardware. If this gun couldn't be made on cost – and be made to *work*, damn it – they'd say so. They didn't get where they were today by giving the go-ahead to a bunch of dud projects, even if they did bring in millions on a cost-plus basis.

This was the all-star team, on whom the Defence Department (and Congress, and the nation) depended for a reasoned, measured, expert analysis. They convened for six months. They made special trips to Aruba, to assure that their impartiality wouldn't be marred by fatigue or tension. They found that a 'ray-gun-type weapon such as that depicted on *Humongor*' could be developed, provided sufficient funding could be obtained to achieve major breakthroughs in one hundred and fifty-two basic technologies.

Other numbers soon followed. Initial estimates for research, prototype development and testing came in at around fifty-six billion dollars. Production would run an additional forty billion. The President, who promised a group of third-graders in Moline, Illinois that, once the N.D. was perfected, he would give it to the Russians, went on television to promote the weapon.

Great communicator that he was, he needed only to show a single chart – a picture of a big missile labelled 'Soviet Threat' beside a smaller missile labelled 'U.S. Capability'. He called for the American people to urge their representatives to approve funding for the N.D. We had fallen behind in defence, he said, but now we were coming back. This was all we needed to even the score.

Yes, the Soviets might be nervous, watching us develop it. But if they could just be patient and let us finish, we'd let them have it, too. They would simply have to trust us. We did not trust them – that's why we needed the weapon in the first place – but then, they knew, as we knew, that

175

we were worthy of their trust in a way that they were not worthy of ours. It all came down, the President supposed, to the fact that everybody in the world, including the Russians, knew that *we were better than they were*. It was on that basis that we could develop the N.D., give it to the Russians, and all live in peace.

Americans define expertise as someone telling them something they don't understand. They didn't understand what the President said and so assumed him to be an expert. They did as he requested and urged Congress to approve the funding.

But Congress wasn't to be so easily bullied. They had the power of the purse, and by God they meant to use it. The President might frighten or snow or otherwise bamboozle the great unwashed at home into buying his bill of goods, but the men on the Hill (and the women, too) had no intention of acting as that man's rubber stamp. They had a will to assert, too.

They insisted on cutting almost twenty-five thousand dollars off the requested hundred billion. The Secretary of Defence went on *David Brinkley* to predict that the missing twenty-five grand would be regarded by the Soviets as an open invitation to invade and conquer the U.S. Somehow, though, it didn't happen. When this was pointed out to the Secretary, two months later, on *Face The Nation*, he thanked God.

Some leading scientists published detailed articles proving that the weapon required technical capability no one on Earth would have for two hundred years. Other leading scientists showed how, even if it could be developed, it might be easily thwarted using off-the-shelf technology. (One article, by a high school senior from Pasadena, proved that an effective shield against the N.D. could be contrived with a sheet of waxed paper and a Pez dispenser.) The Government Accounting Office reported that the N.D. funding would harm the economy and inflate the deficit. The National Academy of Sciences issued a white paper saying that all the nation's best engineers and theoretical scientists were being wasted developing weapons that might not work and would probably never be used.

All of this dissent was praised by the President as proof that our system was superior to the Soviets', and then discredited or ignored.

The companies awarded the various contracts made a fortune, as did their suppliers, the coffee shops and dry cleaners near their facilities, their pension funds, their children's orthodontists, and enough lawyers to fill the Rose Bowl. The economies of California and Texas flourished, at least in certain areas. Neutron Disintegrator T-shirts sold briskly.

But after five years of top-secret research, a subversive traitor at one of the principal defence firms leaked memos to *The New York Times* revealing that:

1) Test reports for the N.D. had been falsified from the first day. The device, designed to discriminate and intercept flying missiles, had only succeeded at discriminating and intercepting an observer's club sandwich. It had also shot at sea gulls, clouds, a turning Chevron sign, a Frisbee, and three girls on an Army base car-park playing jump rope. (All were unharmed. The Chevron dealer sued for ten million dollars, and settled out of court for six. The girls sued for two million and settled out of court for one-five.)

In order to score some direct hits and bolster morale, the N.D. was fired at 'a fixed, rural-based agricultural structure capable of concealing SS-scale tactical weapons, in a transverse orientation', which was Pentagonese for the broad side of a barn. It missed.

2) The device was so sophisticated it could be rendered inoperative by laughing at it within a radius of five feet. It could not be repaired in the field. Estimated

time in the shop was twelve days.

3) Cost overruns for preliminary tests alone had brought the total tab to 92 billion dollars. When asked by a reporter whether that was too much, the President told a story about the time he was a baseball announcer on the radio and the tickertape had broken. Columnists praised the President's mastery of the media.

4) Assuming the weapon could be made to fire, shooting it even once at full force could, due to some quirk in the nation's electrical power grid, plunge the continental United States into a blackout that would take three weeks to fix. It would be child's play for the enemy to goad us into firing the device at some harmless decoy and, during the ensuing darkness, burglarize the country into submission.

There was an uproar. Indignant newspapers ran editorials demanding to know who had promoted such a thing. (In fact, they had.) Congressmen barked into the microphones of attractive reporters, asking who had voted for such a thing. (In fact, they had.) The President, who the night before had shed tears watching a cassette of Mary Martin in *Peter Pan*, went on TV and asked everyone in the audience who believed in the Neutron Disintegrator to clap their hands. Millions did. Somehow, it didn't help. The project was shelved after an outlay of nearly one hundred billion dollars.

The single prototype, which looked like a bazooka attached to a backpack, was stored at Aerodyne. Phil Blumburtt's friend, Carter, had seen it once. He did not know – no-one knew – if it actually worked. It was still sitting there, on a shelf in a supply cage, beside a half-full 7-Up can and an empty bag of Fritos, when Howard the Duck and Phil Blumburtt burst into the room and descended on the cage doors with sledge hammer and crowbar.

When the doors finally sprang open, Phil rushed in and did a quick inventory of the various devices and weapons gathering dust. Some of them were labelled. He read off each one as he pushed it aside.

'Fur Hat Impaction Grenade . . . Anti-vodka Polarizing Gel . . . Microwave Anti-personnel Blini Simulator . . . Low-yield Onion-dome Pressurization Device . . .' Suddenly he jumped forward. 'Got it!' Howard helped him drag out a shape covered in a tarpaulin. They whipped off the canvas.

'The Neutron Disintegrator,' Phil breathed. 'It's never been fully tested in this form.'

Howard tried to pick it up. Just the complex-looking bazooka half was too heavy, bringing from the duck a sudden squawk. 'Gimme a break –'

'One hundred billion dollars,' Phil said in awe. 'And every penny is right there, in the weapon. A masterpiece of high refined technology.'

'It's too heavy to move –'

'We'll have to modify it.'

He ran over to a power supply cart and found a pair of chain cutters. At long last, they severed his handcuffs. Then, together, grunting and quacking, they hefted the bazooka and its attached power pack onto the supply cart. Howard inspected the controls of the cart as Phil tied down the N.D.

'Is this manual or automatic?' Howard murmured. The cart was one of those little trucklets found in warehouses, with a seat and steering wheel.

'Just be sure to get into firing range without him seeing you,' Phil said. 'One look from his eyes and we're dead. Literally.'

'Right.' Howard idly flicked a lever. 'I'll – KWAAK!'

Wrong lever. The cart took off as though alive, rolling merrily down the hall. With no one at the controls.

Towards the lab.

Somehow, Beverly was getting some energy back. She struggled against the bonds that held her on the table, as Jenning inserted the code/key into the console and the laser spectroscope hummed to life. He looked over at her as the device shifted into position.

'Soon.'

'Soon schmoon, you monster,' she sneered. 'Go ahead – turn me into a Dark Overlord. I'm still gonna spit in your wormy face!'

'We Dark Overlords like a woman with spirit –'

There was a noise. Jenning turned to look and beheld the power cart tootling into the lab, Phil and Howard charging after it. Jenning withdrew the code-key and the machine shut down.

Bev saw them, too. 'Howard! Over here!'

A second later came the crash, as the cart ploughed into a wall and certain possibly essential components went flying. Jenning wheeled slowly and began to hulk towards the source of this distraction in a very menacing and hostile way.

Howard and Phil stared at the cart. It was a mess. Who knew if the disintegrator still worked? They threw debris off it as Jenning moved slowly through the lab towards them.

'I think it's broken!' Howard cried.

'Just get on! Here he comes!'

Phil lifted Howard onto the cart. The duck hit the start lever. It coughed, began to turn over – and then stalled. Just then Jenning appeared. With a cold glare at Blumburtt he raised a hand –

– and, with an explosion of energies Earth physics hadn't heard of yet, the scientist went flying. He landed near some equipment and crawled behind it as Howard cried, 'Philsy!' The duck kept trying to rev the cart but nothing was happening.

'Howard! Jump!' Phil shouted. 'It's not working. Beat it!'

Jenning raised his hand Howard-wards, and another blast gouged a section of wall mere feet away from the frantic fowl. Howard hit the starter again – and it started! He threw it into gear! It fishtailed backwards and swung around, moving smartly in forward.

Howard floored it. 'YAAHOO!'

He zoomed along behind rows of equipment and testing tables. Jenning couldn't keep up, but instead turned in slow, inexorable malevolence, awaiting his opening. Phil, meanwhile, scrambled among the equipment. Jenning spotted him and raised his hand. A bolt of energy flew.

Phil seized a polished reflector (It was right there when he needed it! What an incredible coincidence! Or . . . was it?) and the energy hit him with a physical blow, knocking him back onto his butt. But the mirror had shot back the beam! It exploded in front of Jenning. He staggered, then recovered, and wheeled around. It was the moment's distraction Howard needed. The duck approached at full speed.

Jenning cursed. It was the kind of curse they fling at each other in the Nexus of Sominus, so neither Howard nor Phil Blumburtt quite knew what it meant. But the gas Spewing from Jenning's mouth conveyed unambiguously what must surely have been a similar idea.

'Now die, duck.'

'Come on, baby . . .' Howard patted the barrel of the N.D. (Had he known of its chequered history, he might not have been so confident. What can you expect for a hundred billion these days?) Blissfully ignorant, he found the switch, and fired.

Nothing came out.

The barrel began to turn a cold, translucent blue, but then . . . nada. Jenning, though, raised his hand – and a bolt struck some equipment near Howard in a shower of sparks, flying metal, shattered glass. Howard the More-or-less-fearless Duck swerved the cart and bore down, the disintegrator humming slightly but still emitting nothing.

'This is no longer fun.' Jenning glared and pointed. A bolt unlike any they had seen streaked across the lab at the onrushing duck.

Howard had just enough time to yelp, 'Yikes!' before it hit him.

He took it full force. His body became utterly electrified. He began to shake. His feathers, wildly charged, shot out stiff and apart from each other, like fish skeletons. He became . . . translucent. As Phil and Beverly called out his name, Howard lost control of the cart. It careened wildly, swerving into lab tables, pivoting crazily on its wheels. Howard hung on for more than dear life. He had just enough concentration, communication, command and control to reach towards the other button on the N.D. and aim it at Jenning, just as the creature raised his death-dealing hand for one final assault –

Howard lunged and hit the button.

A jAgGeD *bolt* shot out (!) with an ear-tearing siZZle (!!) and struck Jenning full on (!!!). A ***Light*** more INTENSE than the @@@@SUN ITSELF@@@@ erupted::::::in the ///////centre of the lab///////. It burned for an !instant! – and then [[[[[[vanished]]]]]].

Jenning had disappeared.

But the cart was skidding out of control. Howard covered his face with his arms and leapt! The cart smashed into a wall. There was noise, clatter, small explosions, the sensation of the entire room shuddering as a single structure . . . and then, quiet.

Phil ran over to where Jenning had stood. Howard joined him. They looked around for one wild, baffled second. Then they heard the moaning.

Nearby, on the floor, lay the body of the man Jenning.

A scientist. Who had given his life. Who had made the Supreme Sacrifice, for the cause of Science. Of Research. The Selfless Quest. The Disinterested Inquiry. Into Nature, and so on. So that . . . Man . . . might one day push back the frontiers of Knowledge, or expand the borders of Ignorance, or stretch the envelope of Mind. Mind, I tell you! The Human Mind! So that all men, men and women alike, might live in peace, as brothers. And now he was dead.

Except that, as mentioned above, he was moaning. So that, if he was dead, it was in the mode of being alive. ALIVE! The President would have understood such a thing. Jenning, dead albeit alive, was spent, exhausted, and frazzled as though just electrocuted, but living, and therefore, alive.

'His power must be incredible!' Phil gasped. 'Get the gun – he's still alive!'

'No!' Jenning choked, tried to get up. 'No more power. I'm all right, Jack.'

'Phil.'

'Whatever.' He looked at Howard. 'It was no accident that you were brought to earth, Howard Duck. We were just pawns.' He laughed bitterly. Or perhaps he didn't laugh bitterly. But someone, somewhere, in metropolitan Cleveland or the tri-state area, probably laughed bitterly. 'You and me, Howard . . . You and I? You and me? I? We have been part of some cosmic game of good and evil.'

'I knew it!' Howard said.

'I'm myself now . . . but it's not . . . not . . .'

'Not what, Doc?'

'Not inside me any more – but still here! It's loose. The Dark Overlord is in this room!'

'KWAAK! Where?'

Jenning shook his head.

'Philsy,' Howard said with mounting alarm, 'I suggest we get Beverly and GET THE HELL OUT OF HERE!'

They ran to the table and unstrapped Beverly. She began to speak in a relieved, near-hysterical rush. 'I was so scared! He blew up the smog man! He put his tongue in the dashboard! Then he strapped me here . . .' She faltered, as her gaze was caught by a shape elsewhere in the room. 'Howard . . .?'

He was busy with the straps. 'What'.

'Um . . .' How to put it? 'There's a sort of monster over there . . .' She pointed. He looked.

It was at least seven feet tall: grey, reptilian, with oozing, writhing tentacles. Yet for all its hideousness, there was something familiar about the apparition. Howard was the first to put his finger on it, if only figuratively.

'Am I paranoid,' he inquired. 'Or does that thing look like –?'

'– a duck!' Bev cried.

So it was – the Dark Overlord had selected a new shape to assume, and was slowly transforming itself into a reasonable facsimile of Howard the Duck.

Seventeen

It's taking Howard's shape!' Phil cried.

'KWAAK! I'll murder the bum!' Howard ran towards the Neutron Disintegrator. Too late – the creature snaked out a tentacle and wrapped it slimily around the stout-hearted duck's less-than-plump-and-tender drumstick. The monster yanked and the bird went sprawling.

It began to reel Howard in, dragging him along the floor.

Another lashing tentacle writhed out towards the laser spectroscope and, with the surprising delicacy sometimes exhibited by an elephant's impressively dextrous but, let's face it, somewhat creepy trunk, grasped the code-key and inserted it into the console. The vast machine whined to life, lights flashing, dials registering, laser lasing.

Phil and Beverly ran forward to help Howard. But the creature took notice and sent out two lines of energy. They zipped through the air like superior quality flashlight beams, and struck the somewhat pushy scientist and much-pushed singer. Both were launched instantly into the preliminary stage of dematerialization! Bev and Phil began to shake, helpless within the creature's energetic grip.

Howard saw this over his shoulder, as he was being pulled along the floor to a fate worse even than a career in advertising. He grabbed the leg of a stout lab table, laden with heavy equipment. No good – the table began to creep along with him. The stuff on it began to slide off and cascade all around – various assorted tools, wires, clamps, an axe, a calculator, a –

An axe? In an advanced physics lab?

Howard did not waste time with plausibility inquiries. He was being dragged further away from possible salvation each second. He reached out, straining his duck arm in its duck socket. He had it!

For the past few months Howard had worked at a desk job. He was, inevitably, a little out of shape. But what reserves of energy and flexibility exercise had not provided, terror did: he rolled in a nifty little tuck until he was over the tenacle that so firmly and disgustingly held him, raised the axe, and brought it down with the Quack Fu 'Cry of Unfettered ('EeeeAAAAH!') Releasing'.

The blade sank into the creature's unclassifiable flesh, cutting into the slimy grey matter and releasing an ooze of truly gross green fluid. He whacked again – and the tentacle broke in two. Its grip slackened. Howard wriggled free with a nauseated gulp, and leapt up.

A glance at Beverly and Phil confirmed the stalwart duck's worst fears: they were beginning to disappear from the face of the earth. He flung himself at the power cart and landed squarely thereon. He scrambled aboard and threw the first lever. The Neutron Disintegrator, brainchild of an old man watching cartoons while eating Sugar Pops, hummed to life, the barrel of cold blue, the coils glowing.

The creature detected this; it turned in his direction. Howard had less than a second to wheel the cart into position. He did so. The creature seemed to rear and wind itself up, not unlike frightening Al Hrobosky, the mad Hungarian relief pitcher with the wild hair and Genghis Khan moustache, set to toss a sizzler past some thoroughly bollixed rookie on O-and-2. Howard, a rookie no longer, dug in. He aimed his weapon. He fired.

A brilliant flare of energy shot out of the muzzle and zapped full-bore into the creature! Beverly and Phil staggered, released from its rays, and fell back against the laser spectroscope. Phil looked up and pointed towards the open ceiling and the dawn sky.

'There's more coming down!'

It was true: the device was directing a beam of light towards the heavens. never mind the deeper truth already divined by the alert reader – that a real 'spectroscope' sends out nothing, but in fact is used for *receiving*, for analyzing incoming light, and that therefore – let's not shrink from unpleasant truths – THE ENTIRE STORY OF HOWARD THE DUCK COULD BE SAID TO LACK A CERTAIN DEGREE OF CREDIBILITY. No, there was no time for cheap Debating Society hairsplitting. Down this laser beam of 'mere' light, like firemen on a pole, came sliding three monstrous shapes in the early stages of materialization. They were without clear form – boiling, shifting, inchoate, translucent – but each was growing distinctly more distinct and transparently more opaque.

Phil turned to the duck. 'The machine! Howard! You've got to destroy it!'

'No!' Beverly cried. She opened her hands and pleaded with the bird. '*If you do, you'll never get home!*'

(Jeez, she's right,' Howard thought. 'Wait a minute – WHAT AM I DOING HERE?')

Howard the Duck had reached his moment of truth. In one of those rare, psychologically charged moments of discovery and insight made possible only by the direst of circumstances, time all but halted dead for that darn duck. This dilemma, this choice to be made, hit him with the sudden, retroactively synthesizing impact of a good joke. Meaning; the totality of his whole life, in an instant, quivered on the verge of coalescing into a single unified meaning. It threatened to make complete sense. That was the setup.

His decision, meanwhile, would determine that sense. One way or another, it would be the punch line. From that perspective, Howard (who, despite appearances, had a decent sense of humour) wa able to see clearly and calmly the conditions of his existence and the options they afforded.

For one vibrant second he was not the half-grousing, half-dutiful dodo from the ad agency, part Howard Stoark, part Hatcher in the Rye. He was not the failed med. student, the sometime folk singer, the irascible, disillusioned private citizen, desiring nothing more than to be left alone with a few cold ones and an *Antony Y Cleopoultry*. None of those ducks would ever be faced with this decision. Yet here he was.

But if he was not any of them, who or what were they?

They were costumes he put on and took off – some willingly, others because he felt he had to or, worse, was supposed to. The entire clothes-rack of all those things, and the wardrobe that held them, equalled his puny ego. Ever since he could remember, he had wanted wanted wanted, and been mad mad mad. So he ran around like a chicken with his head cut off, trying on outfits and waiting for the disillusionment that (always, inevitably) followed.

What for for for?

He felt as though he were awakening from a lifelong hypnosis. It was so obvious! There would always be something else to want and someone else to be mad at. If all those roles were merely so many costumes to put on or take off, then all these passionately held attitudes now appeared as simply so many different walls to bang his head against. These precious private desires, these dogged, determined grudges – how (and this was both the best and the worst part) *petty* they all seemed, when compared to the larger imperatives of . . . THE UNIVERSE.

(YES? CAN I BE OF ASSISTANCE?)

(No, thanks. Howard has things under control now.)

An ordinary duck couldn't live his daily life in emotional contact with the larger issues of THE UNIVERSE, true. That was reserved for artists, mystics, and schizophrenics. But what had been Howard's alternatives until now?

Making a 'lifestyle' out of complaining that the world had changed without giving him sufficient notice? Trumping up self-hate as a justification for self-pity?

What gullshit! There were monsters on the loose. When they finished with this world, they would move on to the next. One day they'd land on his. How would he react?

Griping wouldn't help. Snarling that it wasn't his responsibility wouldn't make it. Howard knew that it wasn't fair, that he hadn't created this danger, that he'd been nailed by happenstance, Fate, science, 'progress', history, and bad luck. But what else was new? *C'est la vie – pour touts les canards.*

It took only a heartbeat, but in that packed, pressured, super-conscious moment, Howard was changed for ever. Contrary to the combined momentum of his times, his profession, his peers and his society, Howard made the saving leap: he got out of himself. It hit him like a drug. It totally blew his birdbrain. Finally, at long last, he was through being the duck of the 80s. Howard the Duck became a mensch.

'So long, Duck World,' he murmured, and pushed the button.

X-ray-pumped laser power met neutron-enhanced energy-generation. The reaction occurred on the subatomic level, at the very heart of the conditions that made the physical universe possible. At that unplumbable non-place, where abstract energy congeals – for whatever reason – into concrete matter, where atoms make molecules and molecules make gases, where gases spawn stars, stars planets, planets oceans, oceans amino acids, amino acids life, life cells, cells animals, animals brains, brains minds, minds consciousness, and consciousness ideas, and where ultimately God becomes a scientifically interesting notion, there came a vast unleashing.

Then there was a great big explosion.

The laser spectroscope did not so much 'blow up' as fundamentally change its being, shattering into a trillion flying shards. Its power source melted into a lump the size of a doughnut. Its lenses deliquesced into liquid, then gas, and evaporated. A person hanging around the area would have breathed glass gas. Smoke burgeoned in the lab. The noise spanned the entire audible spectrum and beyond, thundering at the low-end bass (and body-organ jiggling hyper-big wavelengths) until finally whistling away at the highest frequencies with a sizzling, sighing, steamy, evanescing hiss.

Amazingly, neither Phil nor Beverly was hurt. It was astounding. It was unbelievable. They were unharmed. And after an explosion like that. It was truly, truly unusual. Phil – perhaps himself aware of how really, really incredible all this was – stumbled over to Beverly and helped her free of the debris that had, unfortunately, fallen on her in the titanic detonation. 'Where's Howard?' she asked.

They scrambled amid the rubble until they found, protruding from the ashes of his victory, his small duck-hand. They had to dig for his body as though excavating a fossil. When finally he lay revealed, covered in dust and silent and still, they could only kneel in sorrow.

'Howard,' Bev said, choking back tears. 'I don't know where you've gone now . . . but I hope you're happy there. This world treated you badly . . . yet you saved it . . .'

The bird's head moved.

'Howard . . .? Bev said, hoping against hope –

A hideous, hellish voice intoned, 'I'm not Howard any more . . .'

The duck-shape sat up. A single dramatic shaft of light penetrated the clouds of dust and illuminated his/its face: the glowing eyes! The spectral colouring! The slowly opening mouth, now emitting a horrible, otherworldly hissing!

Beverly gasped and withdrew. Phil breathed a heartfelt, 'Oh my God,' and leapt back. The creature was . . .

– coughing?

'Jeez, this dust. Murder on the sinuses.' Howard laughed at their stunned expressions. 'Fooled ya, huh?'

'Howard!' Beverly gasped. 'You're . . .'

'He's –'

'I'm –'

'– UNDER ARREST!'

The voice came from the door: Lieutenant Weber and Hanson, the young cop, stood there. Weber looked – not to put too fine a point on it – lousy.

'On what charge?' Howard demanded.

'Oh, who knows. Maybe you're not under arrest.' Weber came in and surveyed the devastation. 'Maybe I'm under arrest. Who the hell knows any more. All I know is, I'm right back where I started from last night. Wrecked lab and no explanations.'

'Not quite.' Jenning – still alive – had come to, and managed to get to his feet. 'In between last night and now, Howard saved the planet Earth.'

Weber looked at him and said, 'Uh-huh.' He turned to Hanson. 'Get a para-medic in here.'

'For him, sir?' Hanson indicated Jenning.

Weber sat slowly on a stool. It had dawned on him that the paperwork alone on this one would be a killer. 'No. For me.'

'Yes, sir.'

'And Hanson?'

'Sir?'

'Tell him to bring sedatives.' Weber sighed. 'Lots of sedatives.'

'Right, sir.'

The young cop had almost made it out of the door when his weary superior held out his hand and called, 'Oh, and Hanson –?'

'Lieutenant?'

'Better make some strong coffee. I have a feeling we're all going to need some.'

'Right, sir.'

'Oh, and Hanson? Make mine with a shot of Jim Beam.'

The young policeman smiled. 'Yes, *sir!*'

'Better make that a double.'

'*Yes, sir, yes, sir!*'

'Oh, and one more thing.'

'What's that, sir?'

'Better bring some doughnuts. To have with the coffee. Lots of doughnuts.'

The cop grinned. 'You got it, sir.'

'Wait a minute, Weber,' Jenning said. 'What kind of doughnuts?'

The Lieutenant shrugged. 'Who the hell cares? The usual kinds. Crullers and chocolate covered and regular jelly doughnuts. Just do it, Hanson. On the double.'

'Yes, sir!'

'Good.' The young cop started to go. 'Oh, and one more thing, Hanson.'

'Lieutenant Weber?'

'Maybe a few sandwiches. Anybody want some sandwiches?'

'Sure.'

'Why not?'

Howard, Beverly, Jenning, Phil Blumburtt – they all wanted sandwiches. Hanson took orders.

'BLT on white toast.'

'Corned beef on rye?'

'Got it. Mustard? Right.'

'Ham and egg –'

'KWAAK!'

'Sorry, Howard. Make it turkey – no, you know what? Make it a turkey club. I haven't had a turkey club in ten years. Where are you going for the food, Hanson?'

'I don't know yet –'

'Well, my God, wherever you're going, they've got to be able to make a turkey club, don't they?'

'I guess so –'

'Drinks? Anyone want to split something with me? Bev? Split a ginger ale?'

'I'm allergic to ginger, Phil. How about a root beer?'

'Ugh. At this hour? Forget it. I'll have coffee.'

It went on like this for ten minutes. Finally, after he had written down the orders and collected the money, the young Hanson asked, 'Can I get anybody anything else?'

Howard the Duck stepped towards him. 'Yeah,' he said. 'I need one more thing.'

'What's that, Mr Duck?'

'Get me a box of cigars. Something decent.'

The policemen looked quizzically at Weber. 'Sir? Are we authorized to –'

Weber smiled. 'Get Mr Duck whatever he wants, Hanson. After all –' And here the elder cop could not suppress a shrug, and a certain note of grudging credulity crept into his voice as he conceded, 'I guess maybe he *did* save the planet Earth.'

The young officer snapped off a smart salute, not unlike the one the President snaps off at the marines standing at attention as he leaves the Presidential helicopter after the latest Presidential vacation. 'YES, SIR!' Hanson made for the door.

'Oh, and Hanson –?'

'Sir?'

'Be sure to bring napkins. Lots of napkins.'

'Right, sir.'

'You know,' Phil Blumburtt said, 'Try to get those little disposable wet towelettes. Where do you get those? Chicken places have them, right?'

'Rib places, too.'

'Anywhere you eat stuff with your hands, I guess.'

'Well, no. I mean you can't get them at burger places –'

'We have paper towels in the rest rooms here. That'll do, won't it.'

'Sure. Get a move on, Hanson.'

'Yes, sir!'

'Oh, and Hanson . . .?'

'Sir?'

'Um . . .' Weber looked at the others. 'Have we forgotten anything? Food, doughnuts, coffee, bourbon, cigars, napkins, para-medics, sedatives –'

'Maybe a morning paper. See what's going on in the world.'

'See if you can get a *Plain Dealer*, Hanson.'

'Yes, sir!'

'And maybe a *Wall Street Journal*.'

'At this hour? Where do you think you are? New York?'

'You know what's supposed to be a good paper? *The Christian Science Monitor*.'

'Are you kidding?'

'No, really. Amazing, huh?'

'I don't believe it.'

'No, he's right. I heard that too. See if you can get a *Christian Science Monitor*, Hanson.'

'Yes, sir!'

'Oh, and Hanson . . .?'

The young officer paused. 'Sir?'

'Um . . .' Weber scratched his head. 'Jeez, I forgot. Oh. Right. Make it snappy. The press is going to be here soon and I want that Jim Beam before I have to talk to those vultures.'

The cop grinned. 'Yes, sir!'

'Hey, some of my best friends are vultures,' Howard said.

'I'm speaking figuratively.'

'So what? Don't be a speciesist.'

'Okay, okay. Sorry. Get a move on, Hanson.'

'Yes, sir!'

'ENOUGH WITH THE YES, SIR!' Phil Blumburtt shrieked. 'JUST GO!'

Eighteen

The crowd went nuts at the club the next night. With the first tune, Beverly and Cherry Bomb had them in a rock 'n' roll frenzy. From the stage, through the smoke and glare, Bev could see that the kids were a lot more rabid than usual. Their slack-jawed, dead-eyed expressions were informed by that subtle spark of intensity that, among today's youth, denotes interest, rather than the various endemic states of intoxication, boredom, or mental dysfunction.

There was a lot of dancing, too, although less among the stud-and-chain heavy metal working class contingent, than the nice-sweet-kids from the 'burbs. Among these, the boys looked defiantly dorky in tight jeans and math-major short-sleeved shirts, skinny neckties, crew cuts, and ludicrously baggy sport jackets. It was as though a high school phys. ed. class had been bussed to a Proper Attire restaurant, and forced into whatever Size 44 Long sport coats were on hand.

The girls, meanwhile, created a mood half sock-hop, half punk rock heaven, in mock-50s skirts, clam diggers and blousy sweaters, pseudo-promworthy chiffon party dresses, shifts, jumpers. Kids' clothes these days suggested the mass scavenging of a costume warehouse after a nuclear cataclysm had destroyed forever the idea of progress. Add to that the lurid Cover Ghoul makeup, bouncing off-centre pony tails, junky costume jewellery and sneakers, and the vista before Bev and her colleagues equalled a convention of little sisters trying on Mommy's old duds, then dancing with their demented Mormon missionary brothers.

'AWRIGHT!' Ronette yelled between songs. 'Got some hot stuff tonight!' As the audience cheered back, Ronnie made a face at Caldonia, who shrugged. Neither could really explain why the kids were so receptive. There had been other nights when the band had played better than this – and they'd got polite claps and some yawns in their faces. Still, why worry? This was great. 'I could learn to like this,' Ronette muttered to K.C. as they charged into their next number.

An artistic performance is a complex thing; the conditions contributing to its success or failure are unpredictable and usually – alas! – uncontrollable. Perhaps no one will ever be able to explain satisfactorily why Cherry Bomb went down so well that night. Maybe it had something to do with the weather. Or with the new material the 'girls' had been working on.

Then again, maybe it had something to do with the mood across the entire nation.

Because there was, undeniably, something new and wonderful in the air, all across America. After one decade of nothing being okay and another decade of everyone hoping that at least *they* were okay, suddenly *everything* was okay. Better than that, everything was okay *again*.

You saw it on television, you read it in magazines. You heard it in the speeches of politicians and other commercials. It was okay to be American again. It was okay to be (so-called) 'selfish' again. It was okay to want all the things and act in all the ways that for the past twenty years it hadn't been okay to want and act again.

What a time to be alive! It was okay to live in Cleveland again. It was okay to be in a rock band again. It was okay to be a woman again. It was probably even okay to be a duck from another planet again.

Sure, there were problems – spreading poverty and rampant illiteracy, and so forth. No one except lawyers could afford to buy a house. You had to rob a Brinks truck to

197

send your kid to college. The cost of a week in the hospital equalled the G.N.P. of Peru. But it was okay – again – that there were problems like those.

It seemed miraculous, but somehow – after twenty years of assassinations, social conflict, student riots, police brutality, futile slaughter, political scandal, crippling inflation, record unemployment, a declining standard of living, environmental disaster, proliferating terrorism, the concentration of more and more wealth in fewer and fewer hands, and a burgeoning class of the poor and the destitute – somehow, the pride was back!

Certainly Beverly and Cherry Bomb played with more of the pride. Either that, or with more volume. But no, why be cynical? That increased verve and conviction in their performance came from something other than turned-up amps. It came from turned-up pride – because they were artists and artists were, by and large, poor. It was chiefly among the poor that the pride was back. The poor had lots of the pride – it was the only thing they had lots of. As for the rich, well, the pride wasn't all that back among them. It was sad, really. Maybe it was because the old rich didn't need the pride, while the new rich were too busy mimicking the old to afford it.

No, once again the rule of thumb was, the people who had the least to be proud of had the most of the pride. Actually it didn't make sense. But this was America: it was okay again that stuff like that didn't make sense.

Maybe that was why the band sounded so damn good.

Or maybe it just had something to do with the fact that Ginger Moss was gone. In fact he was completely forgotten, both by the girls in the band and by everybody else. Released from the unmediated sleaze of his managerial embrace, the group played with a new feeling, a new sense of dedication, and a brand-new commitment to quality. Quality in music. Quality in lyrics. Quality in yelling semi-obscene taunts back at its audience.

198

Plus these girls were women, which was significant. They were responding to a felt need – the need to eat food, and the need to pay rent. It was the same felt need the likes of which was sending other working women – singles, marrieds, working mothers, unmarried mothers, unmothered singles, mothered workers, married singles, and unsingled marrieds and their mothers – back into the marketplace. Like Beverly, Caldonia, K.C., and Ronette, these were women who were happy to work for an economical fraction of what a man would get – and to get it for doing precisely the same work.

Maybe all this played its part in the new, improved sound of the unfortunately named rock group known as Cherry Bomb. But maybe – just maybe – it had something to do with the fact that Beverly Switzler now played with a newfound knowledge.

She played like a woman who knew what it meant to live on the Edge. She played like a woman who knew what it meant to dig down deep and find the best in herself. And, most importantly, she played like a woman who knew what it meant to cringe in mortal terror while an inter-stellar space-demon shoves his three-foot tongue in a dashboard and then annihilates an entire smog inspection station.

Those were the kinds of dues that didn't go down on the street everyday. You came back from an experience like that, it changed the way you played guitar. And it communicated itself to the other members of the band, too. So maybe that's why they sounded so good.

Then again, maybe it had something to do with the inspiration of the group's new manager.

'You may not know it!' Beverly told the ranting, raving audience. 'But yesterday Cleveland was almost totally destroyed!'

The crowd cheered lustily. Nothing appealed to them more than the prospect of their hometown being laid waste – particularly while they were still in it.

'But Howard the Duck saved it at the last minute!'

There was a loud, heartfelt chorus of boos, curses, other verbal abuse. Bev waved it off and gave Cherry Bomb the downbeat. The girls rocked out.

Backstage, Howard the Duck groused and chomped on his cigar. He turned to the lighting and effects man, Phil Blumburtt.

'What did you say this brand was?' he snarled, looking at the stogie.

'White Owl.'

'Oh.' Howard frowned. He liked the name. 'Well. I've had worse.'

'Glad you like it.'

Wait a minute. What was Phil Don't-Call-Me-Carl (Sagan)-Junior Blumburtt doing here! Had he actually made the leap from palaeontology to rock 'n' roll? Had our humming, bumbling Blumburtt Blumburtt rejected the rigid, reserved world of grownup western science for the wicked embrace of forbidden childhood pleasures, the Lolita of rock 'n' roll? Was Phil throwing over a fine (if nascent) career, in order to stick with his pals, get funky, and play loud nasty music?

Fat chance. The day Phil Blumburtt left anthropology would be the day Steve left Eydie. No, Phil was just helping out, having a little fun before the impending grind of agents, lawyers and deals. He had already written six drafts of a small but scathing speech he intended to read to Dr Chapin, each ending in the same two-word invitation to perform what one didn't have to be a physical anthropologist to know was an anatomical impossibility. Tonight was for fun.

So when Howard the Duck gestured towards the stage and said, 'Okay, hit the strobes and bring in the smoke,' Phil did.

Howard snorted as the strobes flashed in their cold, eye-dazzling, epileptic-fit-inducing rhythms, and smoke began to surge in from the wings. It wasn't enough to just play good rock 'n' roll any more, he thought. You had to turn a concert into a movie. Meanwhile movies came more and more to resemble television, while television was more and more like comic books. God knew what comic books were like these days.

'What are they doing?' he griped, pointing to the band. 'The tempo's all messed up. Didn't we go over this a million times today?'

'Howard,' Phil said. 'If you think it's so easy, let's see you do it.'

The duck hesitated only a second. Then he tore off his jacket. 'Gimme a mike.'

Phil plugged one in and tossed it to him. It was a big mistake. Certain connections in the P.A. system had been overtaxed, probably due to the recent operation of the Neuton Disintegrator at a distance not too far from the downtown club. The whole country had been spared a blackout – the machine had been incapable of firing at full power when Howard had used it – but some of the older electrical systems in the greater Cleveland area had been sorely strained.

Thus it was that when Howard caught the mike, he found himself flying out over the stage, eyes bugging and feathers fried, rigid in the sudden zap and jangle of imminent electrocution. Naturally, the crowd – adolescent sadists to a man – loved it. They cheered his name. Some of them even forgave him for saving Cleveland.

He managed to fling the mike out of his shuddering hand; without its electro-mechanical writhing, he landed on the stage while the band played on. The crowd laughed. The girls laughed. Even Beverly laughed. Howard went into his distinctive slow burn: brows ferociously furrowed, cigar up at an angle in his gnashed teeth, fists clenched. He glared at Beverly.

'What's so funny?' he snarled.

She was able to keep playing while she leaned down and said, 'You are, ducky.' Then she kissed the stupid duck on the head.

Well. Go be mad after that. Howard, who two days before might have stormed off in either a massive sulk or a tooth-grinding rage, now enjoyed the benefit of his expanded philosophical perspective. He got a few yuks at his own expense. 'You're right,' he said.

He bowed as the young hoodlums cheered, and when the mike had been fixed he showed them some Duck World boogie.

He did his Michael Quackson quick-step. He did some stuff he picked up from Roger Poultry and The Hoot. He did his Duck Berry walk. He did some moves he'd seen years ago, before half his audience had been born, at a concert by Ike and Tina Turtle. The kids ate it up.

This sure beat the ad game. And if he might never get back to Duck World, Howard – at least for now – felt alive and loved and grooving.

So he was a castaway. So he was an exile. So he had been ill-treated by certain parties and not left alone by others. So he never felt quite at home, never was able completely to relax, could never quite be sure what the future held.

Howard smiled at Bev and spun the mike on its cord, lofting it into the air and catching it as it fell. He squawked ('SKWAWWWKKK!') and pointed at the crowd as he got down! Down! Down! Figuratively. And then physically, as he went into a sudden split, arms up, hands extended. Gorgeous. The crowd roared.

So he was trapped in a world he never made.

Who isn't?

Stephen Donaldson

The Chronicles of Thomas Covenant, the Unbeliever

'Comparable to Tolkien at his best . . . will certainly find a place on the small list of true classics.' *Washington Post*

'An irresistible epic.' *Chicago Daily News*

'The most original fantasy since *Lord of the Rings* and an outstanding novel to boot.' *Time Out*, London

'Intricate, absorbing, these volumes create a whole new world.' *Sunday Press*, Dublin

The First Chronicles of Thomas Covenant, the Unbeliever

LORD FOUL'S BANE
THE ILLEARTH WAR
THE POWER THAT PRESERVES

The Second Chronicles of Thomas Covenant

THE WOUNDED LAND
THE ONE TREE
WHITE GOLD WIELDER

FONTANA PAPERBACKS

Gerald Seymour

writes internationally best-selling thrillers

'Not since Le Carré has the emergence of an international suspense writer been as stunning as that of Gerald Seymour.' *Los Angeles Times*

HARRY'S GAME
KINGFISHER
RED FOX
THE CONTRACT
ARCHANGEL
IN HONOUR BOUND
FIELD OF BLOOD

FONTANA PAPERBACKS

Desmond Bagley

– a master of suspense –

'I've read all Bagley's books and he's marvellous, the best.' *Alistair MacLean*

FONTANA PAPERBACKS

Fontana Paperbacks: Fiction

Fontana is a leading paperback publisher of both non-fiction, popular and academic, and fiction. Below are some recent fiction titles.

- ☐ HEAVEN Virginia Andrews £2.75
- ☐ THURSDAY'S CHILD Helen Forrester £1.95
- ☐ THE EXILE Peter Essex £2.75
- ☐ BANNISTER'S CHART Antony Trew £2.50
- ☐ WHERE LOVE RULES Elizabeth Nell Dubus £2.95
- ☐ THE LANDOWER LEGACY Victoria Holt £2.95
- ☐ WILD ABOUT HARRY Paul Pickering £2.50
- ☐ FIELD OF BLOOD Gerald Seymour £2.75
- ☐ KING'S CROFT Christine Marion Fraser £2.95
- ☐ THE MORNING TIDE Audrey Howard £2.95
- ☐ THE HUNT FOR RED OCTOBER Tom Clancy £2.95
- ☐ PROFIT WITHOUT HONOUR Tom Keene £2.95
- ☐ RIDE A PALE HORSE Helen MacInnes £2.75

You can buy Fontana paperbacks at your local bookshop or newsagent. Or you can order them from Fontana Paperbacks, Cash Sales Department, Box 29, Douglas, Isle of Man. Please send a cheque, postal or money order (not currency) worth the purchase price plus 15p per book for postage (maximum postage is £3.00 for orders within the UK).

NAME (Block letters) _____

ADDRESS _____

_____